Good and Evil

Other books by Anthony S. Mercatante

The Magic Garden: The Myths and Folklore of Flowers,
Plants, Trees, and Herbs

Zoo of the Gods: Animals in Myth, Legend, and Fable

The Harper Book of Christian Poetry (*editor*)

Contents

GOOD AND EVIL

Mythology and Folklore

Anthony S. Mercatante

ILLUSTRATED BY THE AUTHOR

Harper & Row, Publishers

New York, Hagerstown, San Francisco, London

Designed by Lydia Link

Library of Congress Cataloging in Publication Data

Mercatante, Anthony S
   Good and evil.
   1. Good and evil. 2. Mythology. I. Title.
BL325.G58M47 1978   291.2   77-11809
ISBN 0-06-012968-9

78 79 80 81 82 10 9 8 7 6 5 4 3 2 1

*For my sister Josephine,
my niece Monica,
and my nephews Stephen, James,
and Anthony.*

*"What? shall we receive good at the hand of God,
and shall we not receive evil?"*

JOB 2:10

Chapter 19

Voodoo Mythology and Folklore 173

Voodoo, the popular name for Voudun, has two prominent cults, Pétro and Rada, representing the demonic and beneficent forces in the world.

Foreword

WHERE DOES EVIL ORIGINATE? Who or what is its cause? These and similiar questions have intrigued man's imagination from ancient times to the present day. Every culture deals with the problem in its mythology and folklore. The present volume is an attempt to give a world view to the subject. As the title indicates, this volume deals with mythology and folklore. It is not a study of philosophy or theology, nor is it concerned with the occult. Often, however, myths and folkbeliefs contain religious beliefs or doctrines. The line between mythology and theology, therefore, is very thin. One man's theology is another man's mythology. In this book the comments about theology and philosophy, when they appear, are there as a cultural framework to the myths, folktales, legends, and fables. There may be some professing Christians, Jews, Moslems, Hindus, and Buddhists—to name the major religions whose myths are dealt with in this book—who may object to my presentation. If I have misunderstood some point of doctrine or belief, or offended any sensibilities, I apologize, since it was not done in malice. I hope that charity, professed by all the major religions, will prevail in reading my work.

I would like to take this opportunity to thank all those who have in some way contributed to the book. First, my editor, Harold E. Grove, for his belief in the work and his comments; my sister, Josephine Abbananto, who suggested I write the book; Robert Hawthorne Smyth and Richard Stack, who listened and commented on many chapters; Roger Corless, Associate Professor of Religion at Duke University, who read the chapters on the Orient; Professor Ronald Suter of Fairleigh Dickinson University, who did the research and comments on the chapter on Africa; John C. Spina, who always supplied aid; Louis Untermeyer, who has continually supported my work; Father Donald E. Page, who read and commented on the galleys; Jack Haber, for his editorial advice; and J.B. Singer, who painstakingly read, edited, and commented on the work. I wish also to thank Joseph Montebello of Harper & Row, whose interest in my works as well as complete control over the production of the book was always reassuring. I wish to thank Gary-Gabriel Gisondi, who compiled the index, Milly Matacia, who took my photograph for the jacket, and Susan Ann Protter.

Anthony S. Mercatante

Prologue

A HERMIT LIVED IN THE FOREST, and the wild animals were not afraid of him. He and the animals used to talk together and they understood one another. One day the hermit lay down under a tree, and a raven, a dove, a stag, and a snake came to the same place. The animals began to discuss why Evil should exist in the world.

The raven opened the discussion. "It is all because of hunger that there is Evil in the world. When we have as much food as we want to eat, we sit by ourselves on the bough and caw, and everything is fine. But some other days we are starving and everything looks the opposite, so we can't see the brightness in God's world. Instead, we feel full of unrest. We fly about from place to place, but there is no rest for us. Even if we see some meat afar off, it only makes the matter worse. For if we fly down to get it, either sticks and stones are thrown at us, or wolves and dogs chase us, and we are killed. How much trouble comes upon us from hunger! All Evil is caused by it."

"In my opinion," the dove replied, "Evil does not arise from hunger, but it all comes from love. If only we lived alone, we should have little trouble. Wretchedness shared makes one doubly wretched. Even so, we always live in pairs, and if we love our mates there is no peace for us at all. We are always thinking, 'Does she have enough to eat? Is she warm?' And when our mate is away from us anywhere, then we are wholly lost. We cannot help worrying all the time, 'If only the hawk does not carry her off, or men make away with her!' And we ourselves fly off in pursuit of her, and perhaps find the poor thing either in the hawk's claws or in the snare. And if our mate is lost, then there is no more comfort for us. We cannot eat, we cannot drink; we can only fly about and mourn. How many of us have perished in this way! No. Evil does not come from hunger, but from love."

"No," retorted the snake. "Evil arises neither from hunger nor love, but from ill temper. If we lived peacefully, we should not do so much harm. Everything would be delightful for us. But now if anything is done to us, we fall into a rage, and then there is nothing gentle about us. We think only how we can avenge the wrong. We lose control of ourselves and hiss, and try to bite someone. We would not have pity on anyone; we would bite our own father and mother! It seems as if we could eat our own selves. The moment we begin to lose our temper, we are undone. All the Evil in the world arises from ill temper."

"No," the stag responded, "not from love, and not from hunger or ill temper arises all the Evil that is in the world, but Evil arises from fear. If it were possible for us to live without fear, all would be well with us. We are swift-footed and have great strength. With our antlers we can defend ourselves from little animals and we can run from the large ones. But it is impossible to escape fear. Even if it is only the twigs creaking in the forest, or the leaves rustling, we are all atremble with fear, our hearts beat, we instinctively start to run, and fly with all our might. Another time a hare runs by or a bird flutters or a dry twig crackles, and we think it is a wild beast, and in running away we really fall into danger. And again, we are running from a dog and we come upon a man. Sometimes we are frightened and start to flee, we don't know where to, and we roll over a precipice and perish. And we have to sleep with one eye open, with one ear alert, and we are always in alarm. There is no peace. All Evil comes from fear."

Then the hermit said, "Not from hunger, nor from love, nor from ill temper, nor from fear come all our troubles. But all the Evil that is in the world is due to our different natures. Hence come hunger and love, ill temper and fear."

This fable, *Why There Is Evil in the World,* by the great Russian novelist Leo Tolstoy, places Evil as part of the cosmic order of the universe, making it an integral part of life. What is Evil for one creature is not necessarily Evil for another. The dove who is eaten has fallen on Evil days, but the animal or person who eats the dove has fallen on a Good day. This simplifies the problem, yet presents the basic issues: What is Evil? How does it arise? Is there a difference between Good and Evil?

For a person brought up in a Western tradition such as Judaism or Christianity, the problem of the origin of Evil is very acute. Both these religions and Islam, which is related to them, are monotheistic. They teach the existence of One God who rules and controls the universe. Judaism and Christianity, then, are not philosophical systems, but beliefs grounded in the mighty acts of God as revealed in history, such as in the Exodus from Egypt or the Resurrection of Jesus. Since they teach One True God, how does he, since he acts in time and history, permit the existence of Evil in a world he created and "saw that it was good"? (Gen. 1:18)*

The Old Testament is quite emphatic in its answer. In *The Song of Moses* in Deuteronomy 32:39 RSV, we have:

> See now that I, even I, am he,
> and there is no god beside me:
> I kill and I make alive;
> I wound and I heal;
> and there is none that can deliver out of my hand.

---

*Unless otherwise indicated, Biblical quotations are from the King James Version. Sometimes, however, the traditional "the Lord" has been changed to "Yahweh," a Hebrew name for God.

These awesome words, placed in the mouth of Yahweh, present God as totality, the beginning and the end of all things. It is an image which much of mankind would prefer to forget, for if we credit God with all Good things, we must also credit him with Evil ones.

For example, in the Old Testament there is no concept of demons in the sense of preternatural powers that can intervene in man's life; the Old Testament attributes all man's misfortunes to God, not to demons. God sends his angels as messengers to do his will, either for Good or for Evil. Thus we have in I Samuel 16:14, "But the Spirit of the Lord departed from Saul, and an evil spirit from the Lord troubled him."

As the concept of God became more transcendent in Judaism, however, God was removed from the center of action, and the angels, both Good and Evil, became more prominent. They acted for God. In part of the Old Testament Apocrypha and in Rabbinic literature, demons play an important role. In Rabbinic writings they live in unclean places, experience sexual desires, and are set on destroying mankind. They are frequently called "unclean spirits," which was also the term used by many New Testament writers to describe them.

In the New Testament the Kingdom of God is at odds with the Kingdom of the Devil, who rules this world. The one who frees mankind from the power of Evil (which is often identified with death in Christian thought) is Jesus, the Christ, the Messiah, the Savior. This was achieved by the power of God when he raised Jesus from the dead.

In his letter to the Romans, Paul described Adam, the first man who fell from God's grace by eating the forbidden fruit: "Adam prefigured the One to come, but the gift itself considerably outweighed the fall. If it is certain that through one man's fall so many died, it is even more certain that divine grace, coming through one man, Jesus

Christ, came to many as an abundant free gift." (Romans 5:15, The Jerusalem Bible)

What is the fall that Paul refers to in this passage? It is the myth of Adam and Eve as found in the Hebrew book of Genesis which opens the Bible. Through Adam's act of disobedience to God, he and all mankind were punished. For many Christians the taint is expressed in the concept of Original Sin, an inheritance from Adam on all mankind. The setting of the myth is a garden created by Yahweh for the enjoyment of man. Adam may have and enjoy all that is in the garden.

"Of every tree of the garden thou mayest freely eat," Yahweh God said to Adam. "But the tree of the knowledge of good and evil, thou shalt not eat of it: for in the day that thou eatest thereof thou shalt die." (Gen. 2:16–17) Adam, prompted by his wife Eve (we must remember that the written narrative comes from the hand of a man), who has been tempted by a serpent, ate the fruit of the tree of knowledge. "And the eyes of them both were opened, and they knew that they were naked; and they sewed fig leaves together, and made themselves aprons." (Gen. 3:7)

What is the reason given for the foolish act of Adam and Eve which deprived them of life in the garden? It is simply stated in Genesis, they both wished to be as God or gods, "knowing good and evil." (Gen. 3:5) Man placed himself in the role of God—and since he is not God, but merely a mortal creature, he suffers for his right to defy and reject God. As a result of his action, the writers of Genesis see sin, the cutting off of one's self from God's rule, as the prime mover and cause of all the Evil and misery in the world.

But Paul also believed in the reality of the Devil. He wrote in I Thessalonians 2:18 how "Satan hindered" him in his work and later how the Tempter was out to destroy the work of the Gospel. Paul's belief was shared by the early Christians, who firmly believed in the existence of demons who deceived mankind, leading people astray to worship false gods.

The Old Testament question of why God permits the innocent to suffer was seen in the light of Christ's death upon the cross and his vindication in the Resurrection. Yet the Christians also adopted the Jewish Rabbinic legend of the Fallen Angels to account for the fact that there still were demons in the world. The Fallen Angels were beings who, having free will as men, revolted against God's rule. In some accounts they fell because they had sexual intercourse with humans; in other accounts they revolted out of pride (one of the seven deadly sins). As a result of their rebellion they were cast out of heaven and sent to hell, but they are allowed to wander the earth tempting mankind. This condition will last until the Final Judgment when Jesus with his angels will come and completely destroy them, in Christian belief.

This myth of the Fallen Angels was buttressed in Christianity with a philosophical position which looked upon Evil, and the Evil One, as the Spirit of Negation. This was stated by Saint Augustine, one of the great Latin Doctors of the Christian Church, in his *Enchiridion:*

That which is called evil, when it is regulated and put in its own place, only enhances our admiration of the good; for we enjoy and value the good more when we compare it with the evil. For the Almighty God, who, as even the heathen acknowledge, has supreme power over all things, being Himself supremely good, would never permit the existence of anything evil among His works, if He were not so omnipotent and good that He can bring good even out of evil. For what is that which we call evil but the absence of good?

Augustine's grappling with the problem of Evil was also felt by Maimonides, the great twelfth-century Jewish philosopher. In his *Guide for the Perplexed*, he wrote, echoing Augustine:

All evils are negations. . . . It cannot be said of God that He directly creates evil . . . this is impossible. His works are perfectly good. He only produces existence, and all existence is good. . . . The numerous evils to which individual persons are exposed are due to the defects existing in the persons themselves. We complain and seek relief from our faults; we suffer from the evils which we, by our own free will, inflict on ourselves and ascribe them to God, Who is far from being connected with them.

Augustine set out one of the main Christian statements on the nature of Evil, which was echoed by Saint Thomas Aquinas in such phrases as, "There is a reason behind every Evil" and "God permits some Evils lest the Good things should be obstructed." At the same time, however, amid this philosophical stance these men and their followers firmly believed in the existence of demons who went about the world bringing sickness and death. For many people their philosophical position is much more difficult to accept than the mythological one of the Fallen Angels. To look upon Evil as merely a background to show off Good, to be a setting for the gem of goodness, is of no value, for example, to victims of natural disasters, who are to believe that the destruction of their families and friends was done by God to bring about some Good, or to victims of concentration camps, where Evil is an active reality, having more force than goodness.

The idea of Evil as negation of Good has proved to have a strong hold on Western culture. Dante in *The Divine Comedy* pictures the King of Hell as a three-headed monster, a parody of the Christian Trinity, indicating that Evil cannot create but merely imitate. Goethe, in his epic drama *Faust*, has Mephistopheles say:

I am the spirit that denies!
And justly so: For all things from the void
Called forth, deserve to be destroyed.
'Twere better, then, were nought created.

This speech finds musical expression in Liszt's three-movement *Faust Symphony* inspired by Goethe's work. The last movement, "Mephistopheles," portrays the character of the fiend by a series of grotesque variations upon the Faust theme of the first movement; the Devil doesn't have his own tune, he can only borrow someone else's.

The views so far discussed all deal with patriarchal religions and mythologies, those that envision God in masculine terms. The closest we come to the female image of God in Western culture is in the Christian cult of the Virgin Mary, who combines in her person the many aspects of the ancient mother-goddesses such as the Egyptian Isis or the Near Eastern Ishtar. Mary, however, has only the beneficent aspects of these goddesses; none of their demonic or destructive aspects are associated with her. In Western thought, nevertheless, the demonic aspect was inherited by women, who were seen as vessels of Evil and sin. Saint John Chrysostom wrote, "The woman taught once, and ruined all. On this account . . . let her not teach. The whole female race transgressed." A later Medieval work says, "Adam was beguiled by Eve, not she by him. It is right that he whom woman led into wrongdoing should have her under his direction, so that he may not fall a second time through female levity." Some churchmen even debated whether women could be saved.

Of course the Middle Ages firmly believed in witches, and women were far more often burned than men for demonic deeds, since women were believed more Evil than men because of their lustful natures. Many Medieval woodcuts portray the serpent that tempted Adam and Eve as having the head and torso of a woman.

For ancient people the mother-goddess was both the giver and taker of life, the one who gave joy as well as pain, the one who punished, and the one who rewarded. She expressed in her person that concept of totality similar to the one ascribed by the ancient Hebrews to Yahweh, or in Islam to Allah. One of the best examples of the mother-goddess is found in India, where Mahadevi, the great goddess, combines in her person the totality of existence. Among her many roles are Sati, the good woman, representing the *yoni*, or womb, under which form she is worshiped; Jaganamata, the mother of the world; and Gauri, cow-colored, or brilliant, the goddess of crops. All these manifestations are beneficent. Yet Mahadevi can also display aggressive force, as when she is Durga, fighting off demons, or Kali, the black one, who once almost killed her husband, Siva. Kali appears as a black woman smeared with blood, wearing a skull necklace, corpse earrings, and surrounded by serpents.

Polytheism has the option of dividing Good and Evil between different deities, though it can also ascribe Good and Evil to one deity, as in the case of Mahadevi. When it divides the qualities of Good and Evil, a dualism arises, which finds its clearest expression in Persian mythology.

Ahura Mazda, the Persian god of light, represents absolute goodness, while his brother Ahriman represents absolute Evil. There is no mixture of Evil in Ahura Mazda or Good in Ahriman. The brothers display one of the main motifs found in world mythology—the rivalry between brothers. Biblical examples are Cain and Abel, and Jacob and Esau. Saint Paul, commentating on the tale of Jacob and Esau in Romans 9:4–13, sees Jacob, the younger son, representing the spiritual aspect of mankind, while Esau, the darker, older son, the more animalistic aspect.

The rival-brothers motif is also found in North and South American Indian, African, and Egyptian mythologies. In Egypt, for example, the tale of Osiris, the god of resurrection, and his Evil brother Set follows a drama of betrayal, death, and resurrection which was one of the major myths of ancient Egypt. Yet the duality in Egyptian mythology is not as clear-cut as in Persian mythology. Horus, the son of Osiris who sets out to avenge the death of his father, finally battles Set. But Set is protected by his sister Isis, who is also the wife and sister of Osiris. Horus and Set are then viewed as the two necessary aspects of life, one representing strife, the other peace.

This form of duality is also found in Chinese mythology, in the image of Yin and Yang, the passive and active roles, which are symbolized by one circle having the symbol for both within it. In Japanese mythology the duality is expressed between sister and brother. Amaterasu Omikami is the sun goddess in conflict with her brother. The Japanese myth is associated with a creation myth, as are many of the myths of rivals. One example is Ahura Mazda and Ahriman, who created the world—the former its Good aspects, the latter its Evil ones. Some mythologies, such as the Near Eastern, see the very process of creation as a battle between the forces of Good and Evil. The *Enuma Elish*, the Babylonian poem on the creation of the world, describes Tiamat, the female monster of chaos, and her husband Apsu, the abyss:

There was a time when above the heaven was not named.
Below, the earth bore no name.
Apsu was there from the first, the source of both.
And raging Tiamat the mother of both [heaven and earth]
But their [Apsu's and Tiamat's] waters were gathered
        together in a mass.

Apsu therefore represents the male and Tiamat the female principle of the primeval universe. A battle ensues with the god Marduk, who destroys Tiamat and creates both heaven and earth from her body. Marduk reduces chaos to form earth, as does God in the Old Testament.

In African mythology the sky-god, who is called by many different names, creates the earth but then leaves its maintenance to some other being, a son or lackey, who is blamed for all the Evil in the world, such as death. The introduction of death often comes about by some trick played upon mankind. (Were not Adam and Eve in the Bible myth tricked by the snake?)

The idea of a trick being played upon mankind that deprives people of happiness is found best embodied in the concept of the Trickster, the amoral being who is both creator and destroyer, knowing neither Good nor Evil, yet being responsible for both in the world. The Trickster lacks a moral consciousness and represents perhaps one of man's earliest thoughts on the problem of Good and Evil. The Trickster is often the butt of his own pranks and is punished in the various myths, perhaps because a morally conscious mankind must make the perpetrator pay for his deeds. This motif is found in the numerous mythologies which contain a hell, a place where evildoers are sent for punishment.

These various hells show no limit to man's sadistic imagination, his desire for revenge on those whom he sees as committing Evil in breaking society's taboos. Dante's picture of the torments of hell in *The Divine Comedy* are the best known to Western readers, though Buddhist descriptions of the punishments can match the Christian ones for vividness. To counterbalance the images of hell, various mythologies present a heaven, where the Good are rewarded. Some aspects of Christianity even recognize a middle state, purgatory, where one can work his or her way toward heaven from a state between heaven and hell.

In Islam heaven is a very sensual place, filled with

earthly delights. In Christianity the descriptions are more reticent. The images are of people dressed as angels (which is theologically questionable, since people do not become angels) and playing harps, or of Saint Peter holding a key to the gates of heaven. The absence of earthly images in this heaven of the Christians may stem from Jesus's remark in Mark 12:25 that when the dead rise, "they neither marry, nor are given in marriage; but are as the angels which are in heaven."

Heavens and hells, rewards and punishments, are only part of the answer to the handling of Good and Evil in mythology. Many mythologies connect the end of Evil with the destruction of the world, since so many of them relate the entrance of Evil to the creation of the world.

Differences in approach relate to concepts of time. Judaism, Christianity, and Islam, for example, are based on linear time, a line evolving in history toward the end of the world and judgment. Hinduism, on the other hand, sees life in cyclic time: a creation, a destruction, a creation, and so on. This belief is also reflected in the concept of numerous rebirths; one is born many times. In Judaism, Christianity, and Islam a person passes through this life only once.

Thus Christianity has the image of the Second Coming of Jesus, when he will destroy the Devil, while Hinduism has the last avatar of Vishnu, who is called Kalki, destroy this world and bring about the birth of another. This sense of completing, whether for all time as in the linear concept, or to begin anew as in the cyclic one, expresses mankind's need to encompass as best it can the complexities of existence.

All seem to echo the words of Saint Paul in I Corinthians 13:12: "For now we see through a glass, darkly; but then face to face: now I know in part; but then shall I know even as also I am known."

Chapter 1

Egyptian Mythology

The Good god Osiris and his Evil brother Set act out the drama of betrayal, death, and resurrection for ancient Egypt.

When Osiris was born, a voice was heard to say that the Lord of Creation had come to earth. In the course of time Osiris became the king of Egypt and devoted himself to civilizing his subjects and teaching them the craft of husbandry. He established a code of laws and taught men to worship the gods. Having made Egypt peaceful and flourishing, he set out to teach other nations of the world. During his absence his sister-wife Isis ruled the state. When Osiris returned, his Evil brother Set plotted with seventy-two others and Aso, the queen of Ethiopia, to slay Osiris. The conspirators built a chest according to the measurements of Osiris's body. The box was brought into Osiris's banqueting hall while he was eating, and by a ruse he was induced to lie down in it, whereupon Set and his cohorts closed the box and brought it immediately to the mouth of the Nile, where they set it afloat.

These events happened on the seventeenth day of the month of Hathor, when Osiris was in the twenty-eighth year of his reign. This day was subsequently marked on the Egyptian calendar as triply unlucky, since it was the day Isis and Nephthys (a sister of Osiris and Isis) began their great lamentation for Osiris.

When the report of the treachery reached Isis, she cut off a lock of her hair, which was a sign of mourning, and set out to find her husband's body. In the course of her wanderings she discovered that Osiris had slept with their sister Nephthys and that the offspring of the union was a jackal-headed god, Anubis. Isis found Anubis and brought him up to guard her. (Actually Osiris had not lusted after Nephthys, who was in love with him, but had been unwittingly tricked by his sister into relations with her.)

Isis learned that the chest had been carried by the waves to the coast of Byblos and there lodged in the branches of a bush, which quickly shot up into a large and beautiful tree, enclosing the chest on every side so that it could not be seen.

Because of its unusual size the king of Byblos had the tree cut down and made into a pillar to support a room of his palace. Isis, hearing of this, went to Byblos, where she served the queen's women so kindly that she was taken to the palace and made nurse to one of the queen's sons. She used every opportunity she could to transform herself into a swallow, hovering around the pillar and bemoaning her fate. Every night she put the queen's son into a special fire to consume his mortal parts so that he would be immortal. When the queen happened to see her son in flames, she cried out, depriving the child of immortality. Isis then told her the full story and begged for the pillar that supported the roof. The queen, pitying the bereaved goddess, had the pillar cut open and the chest removed. Isis, upon seeing the body of her dead husband, cried out with such fierceness that one of the queen's children died of fright.

Isis then set sail for Egypt. Upon arriving there, she embraced the corpse and wept bitterly. She then went to visit her son Horus at Per-Uatchit (Butos), first depositing Osiris's body in a remote place. One night while the Evil Set was out hunting, he accidentally found the sacred chest. Knowing whose body was inside it, he tore the box into pieces, fourteen in all, dispersing the parts all over the country.

When Isis heard of this, she took a boat of papyrus, a plant abhorred by the crocodile, and sailed about collecting the fragments of Osiris's body. Wherever she found a part of her husband's body, she built a tomb. It is said that is why there are so many tombs of Osiris scattered throughout Egypt. Isis collected all the pieces of her husband but one, the penis, which had been devoured by the lepidotus, the phagrus, and the oxyrynchus, fish which the Egyptians afterward held in especial avoidance. Isis then constructed a phallus to take the place of her husband's, and a festival was held in its honor.

After some time Osiris's spirit returned from the dead and appeared to his son Horus, encouraging him to avenge his death. (This was done in a manner similar to Shakespeare's *Hamlet*, where Hamlet's dead father urges his son to avenge his murder.) Horus and Set engaged in a great battle that lasted for three days. Horus was the victor, but Isis, taking pity on her brother Set, let him go free. Enraged, Horus cut off his mother's head, which the god Thoth replaced with a cow's head. (Some figures of Isis are cow-headed.) Set appeared before the gods and accused Horus of being a bastard, but Thoth defended Horus, and thereupon two more battles ensued between the combatants in which Horus again proved victorious.

This is the general outline of the Osirian myth as written by the Greek historian Plutarch in his work *Isis and Osiris*. Osiris was the man-god (he was first a human being and later deified) who had conquered death, and so, the ancient Egyptians believed, would his followers. In every funeral inscription from the pyramid texts to the Roman period, what was done for Osiris was also done for the deceased, the deceased being identified with Osiris.

Osiris absorbed the characteristics of so many gods that he became both the God of the Dead and the God of the Living. Originally he may have been the personification of the flooding of the Nile. He may also have represented the sun after it had set, and as such he symbolized the motionless dead. Some later texts identify him with the moon. The Egyptians said that Osiris was the father of the gods who had given birth to him, as he was the father of the past, the present, and the future (immortality).

The Land of the Dead ruled over by Osiris was called Tuat (Duat). Originally Tuat signified the place through which the sun-god, Ra, passed each evening after his setting, or death, on his journey to that portion of the sky from which he would appear the next morning. Although generally called "the underworld," Tuat was not believed to be situated under the earth, but rather away from the earth in a part of the sky where the gods resided. Tuat was separated from the world by a range of mountains that surrounded it, forming a great valley. On one side the mountains divided the valley from the earth, and on the other side, the valley from the heavens. In Hebrew mythology the blessed are separated from the damned by a wall. And in the New Testament (Luke 16:26), Lazarus is separated from Dives in Hell by a "great gulf."

Through Tuat ran a river that was the counterpart of the Nile in Egypt and of the celestial Nile in heaven, and on each bank of this river lived a vast number of beasts and devils who were hostile to any being that invaded the valley. Tuat was further divided into twelve sections, or nomes, each of which corresponded to one of the hours of the night.

According to one Egyptian text, *The Book of Pylons*, Tuat is a long, narrow valley with sandy slopes, divided into two equal parts by a river on which the boat of the sun sails. Each of the twelve sections, or nomes, of the valley has its own demons, or ordeals, that the deceased has to pass through in order to be worthy of life with Osiris. The same concept is used in Mozart's opera *The Magic Flute* (1791), in which the hero Tamino undergoes a series of ordeals instigated by the high priest Sarastro in order to be worthy to praise Isis and Osiris.

Tuat was sometimes called Ta-tchesert, or the Holy Land. Another common name for the abode of the dead in Egypt was Neter-khertet, or Khert Neter, "divine subterranean place."

Set, the brother-opponent of Osiris, was the son of the earth, Geb, and the sky, Nut. At birth he tore himself

violently from his mother's womb. Because of his harsh
and bloody ways, he became an abomination to the people, the personification of drought, darkness, and perver-
sity, and the natural opponent to all that was Good and
life-giving in the universe.

The worship of Set was one of the oldest cults in Egypt.
Originally he was a beneficent god of Upper Egypt, whose
realm was the abode of the blessed dead, where he performed friendly offices for the deceased. When the followers of Horus the Elder, the supreme god of Lower
Egypt, conquered the followers of Set, Set's place in the
Egyptian pantheon fell into disrepute, and eventually the
priests of Horus declared Set a god of the unclean, an
enemy of all other gods, and ordered all his images destroyed.

Set was the archenemy of the sun-god, and almost all
allusions and myths pertaining to him reflect the battles he
waged against the sun. In the earliest and most simple
form of the myth, Set represented the cosmic opposition
of darkness and light. In a later form of the myth, Set was
the antagonist of the sun-god, Ra, and sought, in the form
of the monstrous serpent Apep, to prevent him from appearing in the east daily.

The result was always the same. Apep was annihilated
by the burning heat of Ra, and Set, who could renew himself daily, collected his noxious cohorts and readied himself for the next night's battle against the sunrise. In the
most famous and complex version of the myth as given
above, Set was the murderer and dismemberer of his twin
brother, Osiris, who was often identified with the sun.

Although the ancient Egyptians viewed the battle between Set and Horus as the ultimate victory of Good over
Evil, according to some interpretations, in the sphere of
the eternal, where there is no duality, Set and Horus are
one; that is, death and life, darkness and light are one. In

Egyptian religion this has been referred to as "the secret of the two partners," reflecting the hidden understanding of the two combatant gods. Set, representing strife, is perennially subdued but never destroyed by Horus, representing peace. In the end there is reconciliation. The Pharaoh, who was sometimes known as the Two Lords, was identified with both of these gods as an inseparable pair.

As the great antagonist of light, Set's emblem was the primeval knife, the instrument of dismemberment and death. His female counterpart was his sister Nephthys, who was herself a goddess of darkness and decay. In Egyptian art Set is usually portrayed as a man with the head of a fantastic beast having a pointed muzzle and high, square ears. This unidentifiable beast has been commonly called the Typhonian animal, Typhon being the god whom the Greeks identified with Set. Sometimes Set was portrayed with horns and red hair. When Christianity was preached in Egypt, Set was seen as the Devil, and Osiris, the god of death and resurrection, was viewed as Christlike. This identification was intensified when the *ankh*, the cross of life, which Osiris held in his hands, was viewed as a prefiguration of the cross of Christ.

Chapter 2

Babylonian and Assyrian Mythologies

Ishtar, the great mother-goddess, dispenser of
Good and Evil, and Gilgamesh, the hero-king she loved,
who rejected her, portray man's state of helplessness.

The great goddess Ishtar once looked down from her home in heaven to the deep pit of hell. She decided she wanted to go down but told her minister, Ninshubar, that after she was gone, he was to "beat a drum in the holy shrine" for her sake, telling the gods Enlil, Nanna, Eridu, and Enki that she was in the underworld. Ishtar then went down and arrived at the gate of hell. When its chief keeper, Neti, asked what she wanted, Ishtar lied—telling him she had come for the burial rites of Gugalanna, the husband of Ereshkigal, queen of the underworld. Ereshkigal was Ishtar's sister.

Neti reported to the queen that her sister Ishtar was at the gate of hell and wished to enter. Ereshkigal told Neti to let Ishtar in but to be certain that as each of the seven doors of hell was unlocked, Ishtar followed the rite connected with passage through the gate.

Ishtar then went from door to door. At each door she was divested of some symbol of her power—her Shugurra, the desert crown, her lapis lazuli rod, her necklace, two stones that lay on her breast, her golden ring, her pectoral gems, and finally the "robe of sovereignty that covered her body."

At the last door Ishtar dropped naked onto her knees before her sister Ereshkigal. The queen of hell, in conjunction with seven judges, pronounced the sentence that Ishtar was to die. Immediately the goddess died and her corpse was hung on a pike. Three nights passed. Ninshubar, Ishtar's faithful follower, then did as the goddess had instructed him. He called upon the gods for help, but only Enki responded (in the poem, he is called Ishtar's father). Enki formed two beings, the Kurgarru and Kalaturru, giving the first the Food of Life, and the second the Water of Life.

The two descended to hell, asking for Ishtar's body.

When they found it, they sprinkled the Food of Life and the Water of Life on the body, restoring it to life. But one problem remained—another dead body had to be substituted for the restored one of Ishtar. With characteristic cruelty Ishtar offered her youthful husband, Tammuz, who was then grabbed by seven demons, killed, and taken to hell, where his body replaced that of the resurrected goddess.

A variant poetic version of *Ishtar's Descent into the Underworld* was used by the French composer Vincent d'Indy for his *Istar* (1896), a set of symphonic variations for orchestra. Instead of the main musical theme coming first, it appears only at the end to indicate the complete nakedness of the goddess before the last gate. In d'Indy's text Ishtar descends to the underworld to find her husband, Tammuz. She brings him back to earth because the land is barren without him—he is the spirit, or god, of vegetation.

Ishtar was both a beneficent goddess and a demonic deity. She combined in her person and worship nearly all the attributes, both Good and Evil, of many Near Eastern goddesses. As a beneficent deity she was the "great mother of the gods" as well as the "mother of men." She grieved over people's sorrows, being sung of in one hymn as "she who loveth all men," and in another addressed as the goddess who "lookest mercifully upon a sinner." In this beneficent role Ishtar bestowed life, health, and prosperity with her "life-giving glance." She was the giver of vegetation, the creator of animals, wedlock, maternity, and all earthly blessings and moral laws for humankind.

But alongside her beneficent role, Ishtar was also a demonic goddess. She was the warrior-goddess. A votive tablet placed for the great ruler Hammurabi says, "Ishtar has given the conflict and battle; what more canst thou hope?" Ishtar was also a storm-goddess, "the lofty one who causes the heavens to tremble, the earth to quake

. . . who casts down the mountains like dead bodies."

Since Ishtar combined so many attributes of other goddesses, the myths surrounding her are often in conflict. In one account, for example, she is said to be the daughter of the moon-god, Sin, and sister of the sun-god, Shamash. In another account she is the daughter of Anu, the lord of heaven. Both accounts agree, however, that she is connected with the planet Venus, being called "lady of resplendent light" in that role. Her symbol in this connection was an eight-pointed star, a symbol later associated with the Virgin Mary in Christianity.

Ishtar's most important role was as goddess of sexual love. In this aspect she displayed an extremely despotic attitude. In the Babylonian epic poem *Gilgamesh*, she was at first in love with the shepherd Tammuz, then with a bird, then a lion, then a horse, then a shepherd, then a gardener, and finally with Gilgamesh, the hero-king. Gilgamesh rejected Ishtar because she was responsible for the death of so many lovers.

Gilgamesh was part god and part man. He was a great warrior ruling over the city of Uruk with absolute power, having little or no regard for the welfare of his people. One day the citizens of Uruk appealed for help to the goddess Aruru (a form of Ishtar), who had originally created Gilgamesh. They begged the goddess to save them from the tyranny of the despot. In response Aruru created Enkidu, a being like a man who had hair all over his body and was at home with all the animals:

> Eating herbs with gazelles,
> Drinking from a trough with cattle,
> Sporting with the creatures of the waters.

Enkidu, the natural man, as opposed to Gilgamesh, who had become corrupted by power, freed animals that had been trapped by hunters. Gilgamesh heard of Enkidu and sent a messenger, Sadu the hunter, who was a "wicked man," to ensnare Enkidu. For three days in succession Sadu watched Enkidu drinking at a trough with the cattle, but each time he attempted to catch him, he failed because Enkidu was too quick for him. Sadu then returned to Gilgamesh for further instructions. Gilgamesh told him:

> Go, hunter mine, and take thee Ukhat,
> When the cattle come to the trough,
> Let her tear off her dress and disclose her nakedness.
> Enkidu will see her and approach her.
> His cattle which grew up on his field will forsake him.

Ukhat (Ukhatu) was a harlot dedicated to the worship of Aruru. Following the instruction of Gilgamesh, Sadu took the woman to Enkidu. The woman took off her clothing, exposed herself before him, and "unabashed, she enticed him." The two made love for six days and seven nights. Then Enkidu turned to see his cattle, and "the cattle of the field turned away from him," but Enkidu was "enthralled at the feet of the harlot."

Ukhat then told Enkidu to go to the great city of Uruk, to see Gilgamesh, who was "perfect in power, surpassing all men in strength, like a mountain bull." They arrived to find the city celebrating. Dressed in festive clothes, the young people were dancing in the streets. Surrounded by his court, Gilgamesh made his entrance. The procession stopped in the court of the temple.

As Gilgamesh was about to enter the temple, Enkidu ran up and challenged him to a battle. The two fought. Gilgamesh was forced to the ground. The battle ended when both realized they had met their equal, and they became friends.

Gilgamesh and Enkidu then proceeded to the cedar

forest to battle the monster Humbaba. The cedar forest
was sacred to the goddess Ishtar. Both men attacked the
monster, beheading him. The goddess, impressed by the
strength of Gilgamesh as well as by his daring, decided to
entice him with her sexual charm. She said to him:

> Come, Gilgamesh, be my husband,
> Thy love grant me as a gift,
> Be thou my husband and I will be thy wife.
> I will place thee on a chariot of lapis lazuli and gold,
> With wheels of gold and horns of sapphire.

But Gilgamesh was not moved by the words of the goddess, remembering how she had destroyed all her other
lovers, devouring them with her lust. Determined that
Gilgamesh should not get away from her, Ishtar appealed
to her father, Anu, the lord of heaven, to create Gudanna,
or Alu ("the strong," or "supreme one"), a majestic bull of
heaven. Gilgamesh, with the aid of Enkidu, fought the
celestial creature and defeated him. The enraged goddess
cried out:

> Cursed be Gilgamesh, who has enraged me,
> Who has killed the Divine Bull.

To add to the insult, Enkidu challenged the goddess by
hurling the Gudanna into her face. For this act Enkidu
died. Shaken by his friend's death, Gilgamesh became sick
and tried to seek the secret of immortality, since he did
not wish to die too. He made the arduous journey to the
land where Utnapishtim, the hero of the great Flood, and
his wife healed Gilgamesh by magic food. During this
time Gilgamesh had been in a heavy sleep. When he
awoke, he was not completely cured and Utnapishtim told
him he must bathe in the Fountain of Life. Gilgamesh
went to the place of purification with Utnapishtim's fer-

ryman, Urshanabi; his body was washed in the waters, and his sores and sickness disappeared.

Gilgamesh was now ready to return to his own city of Uruk. At his wife's suggestion, Utnapishtim revealed to Gilgamesh the "secret of life," which was a plant that wounded like a thistle but which restored life. Gilgamesh and the ferryman, Urshanabi, found the plant, which grew at the side or bottom of a fountain. Gilgamesh secured it, but scarcely had his hands grasped the plant when it slipped away and was snatched by a demon-serpent.

Gilgamesh continued to lament the loss of Enkidu, whose spirit appeared and described Aralu, the underworld. Gilgamesh realized that men must die, and even he, a great king, could not escape the universal fate of mankind.

Aralu was pictured as a vast place, dark and gloomy. Sometimes it was called a land, sometimes a great house. To approach it was difficult since it lay in the lowest part of a mountain. Aralu was surrounded by seven walls and guarded so that no living person could enter it and none ever came out. A second name for the land of the dead in Babylonian mythology was Ekur ("the bright mountain house"); a third, Shalu ("to ask"); a fourth, Ganzir, a word whose meaning is uncertain. In numerous incantations the names of the land of the dead were avoided and the place was often described as "land of no return," "dark dwelling," or "great city."

The cruelty of the goddess Ishtar is matched by the cruelty of Ea, the god of the waters, toward Adapa, his son. Adapa was "wise like one of the gods," being under the special protection of his father, the god of the waters and the primeval deep. Ea gave Adapa "intelligence enough to comprehend the design of the world, but he made him a dying man."

One day Adapa went fishing. While he was in the middle of the sea, a storm caused by the South Wind arose, capsizing the boat. In a fit of rage Adapa cursed the South Wind.

"O South Wind," he cried out, "you have overwhelmed me with your cruelty. I will break your wings." (The South Wind is often pictured as a winged bird or monster in Babylonian art.)

As Adapa finished this curse, the wings of the South Wind were destroyed. For seven days (a number which in mythology indicates a rather long though indefinite period) the wind did not blow over the sea or earth. When Anu, the god of heaven, learned of this he called his god, Illabrat.

"Why has the South Wind not blown for seven days across the land?" Anu asked.

"My Lord Adapa, the son of Ea, has broken the wings of the South Wind," Illabrat replied. At this Anu became very angry and commanded that Adapa appear before him. Ea prepared his son Adapa for questioning from the god Anu.

"When you come before Anu, they will offer you the food of death," Ea said. "Do not eat it. They will also offer you the waters of death. Do not drink. They will offer you a garment. Put it on. They will offer you oil. Anoint yourself. Do not forget now what I have told you."

When Adapa appeared before Anu, he did as his father, Ea, had instructed, and refused the food and drink offered, even though Anu said it was the Food of Life and the Water of Life.

After Adapa refused, Anu asked, "Why did you not eat and not drink? Now you cannot live forever, for you refused the food and water of everlasting life."

"Ea, my father and lord," replied Adapa, "commanded

me not to eat and not to drink." Then Anu laughed, for Ea had tricked his son Adapa, keeping for the gods the gift of immortality.

Humankind not only lost immortality through the Evil of the gods, but people also suffered from demons which filled the land to destroy them.

The Babylonians believed that Evil spirits resided everywhere, lying in wait to attack mankind. Each demon was given a name which described its function. Thus *lilu* ("night spirit") and *lilitu*, its female form, indicated demonic spirits that worked their Evil at nighttime. *Eki mmu* ("seizer") was a shadowy demon that hovered around graves waiting to attack any passerby. The *rabisu* ("the one that lies in wait") and *labartu* ("the oppressor") were the demons who gave nightmares to the sleeping. *Ardat lili* ("maid of the night") was a demoness who approached men, aroused their sexual passions, and then did not permit them to have orgasm. Other demons were *akhakhazu* ("the capturer"), *namtar* ("the demon of plague"), *ashakku* (the demon of "wasting disease"), and *namataru*, the spirit of fate, a son of the great god Bel, who executed instructions given him concerning the destiny of mankind.

To protect themselves against these various demons, the Babylonians and Assyrians evolved an elaborate series of incantations to ward off Evil. They pictured demons as monstrous beings having animal heads and human-shape bodies. With gaping mouths and armed with weapons, the *utukku* stood ready to attack their next victim.

Assyrian kings acknowledged the power of the *utukku* by having statues of them placed at the approaches, entrances, and divisions of their temples and palaces. This was done in the hope of securing their protection instead of their vengeance.

The great bulls and lions with human heads often seen on various monuments are part of the same concept.

These colossal statues were known by the name *shedu,*
which is another term for demon. Though the demons assumed animal forms, they could also make themselves invisible.

Since there were so many demonic beings, incantations
often grouped them, as the following famous text, *Seven
Are They:*

> Seven are they, they are seven,
> In the subterranean deep, they are seven,
> Perched in the sky, they are seven,
> In a section of the subterranean deep they were reared,
> They are neither male nor are they female,
> They are destructive whirlwinds,
> They have no wife, nor do they beget offspring.
> Compassion and mercy they do not know,
> Prayer and supplication they do not hear,
> Horses bred on the mountains, are they.
> Hostile to the god Ea are they,
> Powerful ones among the gods are they.
> To work mischief in the street they settle themselves in the
>   highway.
> Evil are they, they are evil,
> Seven are they, they are seven, seven, and against
>   seven are they.

Chapter 3

Persian Mythology and Zoroastrianism

The continual battles between Ahura Mazda, the god of light and goodness, and his Evil brother, Ahriman, are the best-known examples of dualism in world mythology.

Zurvan, the god of time and space in Persian mythology, was the father of the Good god, Ahura Mazda, and his Evil brother, Ahriman. When the two were conceived, Zurvan decided that whichever came to him first would be king. When the Evil Ahriman heard this in his mother's womb, he ripped it open and emerged, coming toward his father. "Who are you?" Zurvan asked.

"I am your son, Ahura Mazda," the Evil Ahriman replied.

"Ahura Mazda is light and you are dark and stinking," Zurvan replied.

While the two were still speaking, Ahura Mazda came out of his mother's womb. Zurvan immediately recognized him and made him king.

"Did you not vow," asked Ahriman, "that whichever of your sons should come first, you would give to him the kingdom?"

"You false and wicked one," Zurvan replied. "The kingdom shall be given to you for nine thousand years, but Ahura Mazda is nevertheless king over you and will triumph after that time."

Ahura Mazda then created the heavens and the earth, and all beautiful things, but Ahriman created demons, snakes, and all Evil.

This myth captures the dualistic nature which is the main characteristic of the Persian mythological worldview. The earth is seen as a battleground in the struggle between the forces of Good and Evil, respectively symbolized by Ahura Mazda and his brother Ahriman. In this struggle Ahura Mazda will be the victor. According to the Prophet Zarathustra, who reformed Persian religion, Ahura Mazda created the cosmic order, the moral and material worlds, and is the creator, sovereign, omniscient god of order. Zarathustra says Ahura Mazda is uncreated and eternal. This view rejects the apparently literal birth of the god-brothers in the myth. In a hymn ascribed to Zarathustra is written:

> O Ahura Mazda, this I ask of thee; speak to me truly!
> How should I pray, when I wish to pray to one like you?
> May one like you, O Mazda, who is friendly, teach
>   one like me?
> And may you give us supporting aids through friendly
>   justice,
> And tell us how you may come to us with
>   Good Disposition?

In a later inscription placed by King Darius I (548–486 BC), Ahura Mazda is raised to the position of the One True God:

> There is one God, omnipotent Ahura Mazda,
> It is He who has created the earth here;
> It is He who has created the heaven there;
> It is He who has created mortal man.

Though so powerful, Ahura Mazda has a host of spiritual helpers, the most important being Amesha Spentas ("immortal bounteous ones"), who are either separate beings from Ahura Mazda or manifestations of himself, depending on the interpretation of the myth.

The first of the seven Amesha Spentas is Vohu Manah, the first-born of Ahura Mazda, who sits at his right hand, protecting animals. He appeared to the Prophet Zarathustra, telling him what Ahura Mazda expected of him. Vohu Manah keeps a record of men's thoughts, words, and deeds, and he acts as a recording angel.

The second of the Amesha Spentas is Asha, the truth, and the most beautiful of Ahura Mazda's creations. She represents divine law and moral order. The faithful in

Zoroastrian belief, for example, are called Ashavans, followers of the truth of Ahura Mazda.

Kshathra Vairya, the third, is a personification of Ahura
Mazda's might, majesty, dominion, and power. He helps
the poor and weak overcome all Evil.

The fourth, Armaiti, devotion, is another daughter of
Ahura Mazda and sits on his left hand, presiding over the
earth and cattle with pasture. She is the personification of
faithful obedience, harmony, and religious worship.

Fifth is Haurvatat, integrity, a personification of salvation, the spirit of health, and protector of water and vegetation.

The sixth is Ameretat, immortality, or deathlessness,
and like Haurvatat is associated with water and vegetation.

The last is Sraosha, obedience, guardian of the world,
who feeds the poor and will later help judge the world.

Equal in rank to the Amesha Spentas is the god of life,
heat, and fertility, Mithras. He is a mediator between the
gods and men, and chief aid to Ahura Mazda in his war
against Ahriman. Mithras's worship, however, was not re-
stricted to Persia. Between 1400 BC and 400 AD, Indians,
Romans, and Greeks also worshiped the god, who may
be the sun-god Mitra mentioned in the Indian collection of
hymns, the *Rig-Veda*.

During Roman times the worship of Mithras was converted into a Mystery Religion under influences drawn
from the Greek philosopher Plato. Mithras was worshiped particularly by soldiers and imperial officials of
Rome. The nineteenth-century singer of Britain's empire,
Rudyard Kipling, in his poem *A Song to Mithras*, captures
the mood of the Roman belief in the god's powers:

> Mithras, God of the Morning, our trumpets waken
>   the Wall!
> Rome is above the Nations, but Thou art over all!

Now as the names are answered, and the guards are
　　marched away,
Mithras, also a soldier, give us strength for the day!
Mithras, God of the Midnight, here where the great
　　Bull dies,
Look on Thy Children in darkness. Oh, take our
　　sacrifice!
Many roads Thou has fashioned—all of them lead
　　to Light!
Mithras, also a soldier, teach us to die aright!

Part of Kipling's poem refers to the oft-repeated theme
in reliefs or statues that depict Mithras. The scene portrays a young man wearing a red Phrygian cap, slaying a
massive bull while a dog licks the blood, a serpent crawls
nearby, and a scorpion seems to be removing the bull's
testicles. On either side of the scene is a young man, one
with a torch uplifted, the other with a torch facing down-
ward.

What exactly this scene symbolizes has puzzled
scholars. The Swiss psychologist Jung, picking up the
similarity between the Mysteries of Mithras and the Mysteries of Christianity, saw the slaying of the bull as "essen-
tially a self-sacrifice, since the bull is a world bull which
was originally identical with Mithras himself. . . . The
representations of the sacrificial act, the tauroctony [bull
slaying], recall the crucifixion between two thieves, one of
whom is raised up to paradise while the other goes down
to hell."

Jung was not the first to recognize the similarities between Mithraism and Christianity. The early Church
writer Tertullian noted that the pagan cult contained baptism and the use of bread, water, and wine consecrated by
priests called "father." He felt these similarities were inspired by the devil who wished to mock the Christian sac-
raments. The French writer Ernest Renan, writing in a

sceptical nineteenth-century tradition, wrote, "If Christianity had been arrested in its growth . . . the world would have been Mithraist."

The Emperor Constantine, who converted to Christianity on his deathbed, suppressed the religion of Mithras, though present-day Zoroastrians still worship Mithras as the chief aid to Ahura Mazda in his war against Ahriman the Evil one.

Ahriman, however, is not alone in the battle, for he has numerous demonic aids, the most prominent being Azhi Dahaka, the archdemon of Persian mythology. He has three heads, six eyes, and three jaws. Azhi Dahaka is imprisoned in Mount Demavend because of a battle he fought with the hero Traetaona in Varena, the heavens. Traetaona clubbed Azhi Dahaka in the head, neck, and heart, but the demon refused to die. Finally Traetaona plunged a sword into the monster's breast. Out of the wound came a host of ugly animals: snakes, toads, scorpions, lizards, frogs. Frightened that more of the same were inside the demon, Traetaona took the body and imprisoned it in Mount Demavend. Here the demon will stay until a time in the future when he will escape to cause havoc in the world, then he will be slain by the hero Keresaspa, who will usher in a new world order.

This final victory of Good over Evil has a rather elaborate timetable lasting 12,000 years which are divided into four segments. From the year 1 to 2999, Ahura Mazda called spiritual creation into being, such as angels, good spirits, and the Fravashia, the spiritual primal images of man. In the second age, from 3000 to 5999, the spiritual creation became material under the rule of Gayomart, the primal man in Persian mythology. Ahriman, however, viewed this development with dismay and planned to destroy it. In the third era, from 6000 to 8999, Ahriman invaded the world and killed Gayomart. Other human beings arose from the spilled seed of Gayomart, thus populating the world. The fourth age, from 9000 to 12,000, is the present age. It saw the coming of the Prophet Zarathustra, who taught the Good religion of Ahura Mazda. Zarathustra's seed is saved in a lake and will, through virgins, bring forth three saviors: Hushedar, Hushedar-mar, and Soshyant.

Hushedar "will bring the creatures back to their proper state," after being born of a virgin from the seed of the Prophet Zarathustra. To prove his mission, the sun will stand still at its noontime position for ten days. For three years men will live at peace and see a glimpse of their future happiness, then Evil will again assert itself, and the second savior, Hushedar-mar, will appear. The sun will stand still for twenty days, men will no longer eat meat, and be even closer to the final victory of Good over Evil. But Evil will again arise in the form of the demon Azhi Dahaka, who will break loose from his bonds in the cave in Mount Demavend, only to be challenged by Keresaspa, a hero in Persian mythology noted for his battles with various demons. When Azhi Dahaka is killed, the final, or third, savior, Soshyant, will arrive. All disease and death will be overcome, the final judgment will take place, and a new world will emerge filled with Good.

Chapter 4

Hebrew Mythology and Jewish Folklore

God in the Old Testament and in Rabbinic writings is
the One, True, and Only God; all other spiritual beings,
whether Good or Evil, are part of his creation and
subject to him.

In one of the most terrifying and at the same time majestic passages in Isaiah (45:5–7), we hear God speak:

> I am Yahweh, and there is none else,
> There is no God besides me:
> I girded thee, though thou hast not known me;
> That they may know from the rising of the sun,
>   and from the west,
> That there is none besides me.
> I am Yahweh, and there is none else.
> I form the light, and create darkness:
> I make peace, and create evil:
> I Yahweh do all these things.

(The Revised Standard Version substitutes, "I make weal and create woe," certainly softening the passage.)

Isaiah's verses present the classic monotheistic doctrine on God's nature: God is one, the creator of all things. Thus Good, as well as Evil, comes from God. Such a statement is too much for many to bear. The philosopher Plato, for example (who of course did not read Isaiah but treated the same question), wrote in *The Republic* (Book 2):

God if he be good, is not the author of all things, as many assert, but he is the cause of a few things only, and not of the most things that occur to men; for few are the goods of human life, and many are the evils, and the good only is to be attributed to him; of the evil other causes have to be discovered.

Plato's inability to accept a God who causes both Good and Evil was shared by later Jewish writings. As time progressed, the Jews developed an elaborate system of angels and demons who did the work of God, removing God from the sphere of human action and placing him in a transcendent position. Thus the following two accounts of the same event in the Bible credit the impetus differently. In the earlier account of II Samuel 24:1 we have:

The anger of Yahweh was kindled against Israel, and he moved David against them to say, Go number Israel and Judah!

The same fact is mentioned in I Chronicles 21:1, which was written later, and we have:

Satan stood up against Israel and provoked David to number Israel.

God has been removed and a spirit, Satan, is credited with the action of Evil. Yet Satan, the "adversary," is part of God's heavenly host, as is clearly shown in the Book of Job. Satan tempts Job, destroying his family and goods, but only with the permission of God. When Job cries out for justice he does not condemn Satan, but God himself:

> I am innocent, but I no longer care.
>   I am sick of living, nothing matters;
>   innocent or guilty, God will destroy us.
> When an innocent man suddenly dies, God laughs.
> God gave the world to the wicked.
> He made all the judges blind.
> And if God didn't do it, who did?
>
>   (Good News Bible, Job 9:21–24)

The concept of Satan as the Devil is not found in the Old Testament, since his role is merely as "adversary." As Judaism developed, coming into contact with many pagan cults, Satan took on more of the aspects we know as belonging to the Devil. By the time of the New Testament, Satan was generally regarded as an Evil demon or the ruler of demons (Matthew 12:24–28): He not only controls the body but also has power over spiritual nature, being called "prince of this world" (John 16:11), and even "god of this world" (II Corinthians 4:4). All these New Testament quotes reflect the current Jewish belief of their time.

Following late Jewish sources in writing *Paradise Lost*, John Milton made Satan the monarch of hell, ruling all the Fallen Angels. His chief lords, all deriving from Near Eastern mythology, are Beelzebub, Chemos, Tammuz, Dagon, Rimmon, and Belial. Satan's character as portrayed by Milton is one of pride and ambition, causing the Romantic poet Shelley to find Satan the hero of Milton's epic poem.

In his *Litanies to Satan* Baudelaire, the nineteenth-century French poet, went even further than Shelley and inverted the roles of God and Satan. The Devil is looked upon as the liberator of man, while God is looked upon as his jailer. Here are some of the litanies:

> O most wise and beautiful of angels
> God, betrayed by fate and deprived of praise
>
> Satan, have mercy on my endless suffering!
>
> O Prince of Exile who though wronged and beaten
> Are yet stronger made
>
> Satan, have mercy on my endless suffering!
>
> You all-knowing, great lord of the nether worlds
> Familiar healer of human woes
>
> Satan, have mercy on my endless suffering!
>
> You, who from Death, your old and able mistress,
> Created Hope—a beguiling madwoman
>
> Satan, have mercy on my endless suffering
>
> Staff of the exiled, beacon of discovery
> Confessor of the hanged and of conspiracies

Satan, have mercy on my endless suffering!

Adopted father of those whom God the Father
In his fury has driven from the earthly paradise

Satan, have mercy on my endless suffering!

(Translated by Gary-Gabriel Gisondi)

Satan, however, is not alone in later Jewish belief. Asmodeus, "the destroyer," the demon of lust, appears in a
late nonscriptural Jewish work, the Book of Tobit, which
is included in the Apocrypha of the Old Testament, but
not counted as part of the Hebrew Bible. In the folktale,
Asmodeus is in love with Sarah, daughter of Raguel. She
had been given seven husbands, and "the evil demon Asmodeus had slain each of them before he had been with
her as his wife." (RSV, Tobit 3:8)

Tobias, son of Tobit, wished to marry Sarah. Aided by
the archangel Raphael, Tobias used a magic charm; he
"took the live ashes of incense and put the heart and liver
of the fish upon them and made a smoke. And when the
demon smelled the odor he fled to the remotest parts of
Egypt, and the angel bound him." (RSV, Tobit 8:3)

According to other Jewish sources, Asmodeus was the
son of Naamah, a mortal woman, and a Fallen Angel or
Adam before God created Eve. In Jewish folklore Asmodeus was responsible for the drunkenness of Noah as
well as the construction of the Temple of Solomon. The
wise king, through the powers of his magic ring, forced
Asmodeus and his devil cohorts to work on the massive
undertaking. Asmodeus was not at all happy and devised a
plan to get even with Solomon. One day the king foolishly
allowed the demon to seize his magic ring. The Evil Asmodeus then hurled the ring to the bottom of the sea, and
Solomon was forced into exile, leaving Asmodeus to rule
in his stead. Solomon, however, recovered the ring when

he found it in the belly of a fish. As punishment for his Evil deed, Asmodeus was imprisoned with his demon-friends in a large jar.

In the story of Tobias, we mentioned Asmodeus's rival, the Good angel Raphael. In Tobit 12:15, Raphael describes himself as "one of the Seven Holy Angels which present the prayers of the saints, and which go in and out before the glory of the Holy One." According to Rabbi Abba in *The Zohar* (a medieval mystical Jewish work), Raphael is charged to heal the earth, "and through him the earth furnishes an abode for man, whom also he heals of his maladies." In *Paradise Lost*, Milton refers to Raphael as "the affable archangel."

The Seven Holy Angels which Raphael mentions are not named in the Book of Tobit, but both Jewish and Christian folklore have supplied them. According to most sources, they are:

Michael ("who is like unto God")
Raphael ("God has healed")
Gabriel ("God is my strength")
Uriel ("the Light of God")
Chamuel ("He who seeks God")
Zophiel ("the beauty of God")
Zadkiel ("the righteousness of God")

The most important of the seven is Michael. In Daniel 12:1, the archangel Michael is "the great prince which standeth for the children of thy people." Thus Michael is considered the guardian of the Hebrew people. In the New Testament (Revelation 12:7) Michael fights the Devil. One of the prayers said after the Latin low mass until 1960 was addressed to Saint Michael as defender against the Devil (the prayer was omitted from the new rite in English):

Holy Michael, Archangel, defend us in the battle; be our protection against the wickedness and snares of the devil. Rebuke him, O God, we humbly beseech thee, and do thou, O Prince of the heavenly host, by the power of God drive into hell Satan and the other evil spirits who wander through the world seeking the ruin of souls.

Even the Koran (Sura 2) mentions Michael, saying, "Who so is an enemy to Allah or his angels . . . or to Michael shall have Allah as his enemy."

After Michael and Raphael, the most important of the seven is Gabriel. He plays a prominent role in the Bible as a messenger of God. He first announces to Daniel the return of the Jews from their captivity (Daniel 8:14) and explains the vision of the various nations (Daniel 9:21–27). In the New Testament, Gabriel announces to Zacharias the coming birth of John the Baptist (Luke 1:11–23) and to the Virgin Mary that she will be the mother of Jesus (Luke 1:26–38).

Milton in *Paradise Lost* (Book 4) calls Gabriel the "Chief of the angelic guards," recalling the Biblical text. Cole Porter in his musical show *Anything Goes* (1934) has a brilliant song, "Blow, Gabriel, Blow," which depicts the angel with a magnificent trumpet and the task of announcing the end of the world.

Uriel, the next angel on the list, does not hold as important a place as Michael, Raphael, or Gabriel, all of whom are named in the Bible, since Uriel is not mentioned in any Biblical text. He is found in the Old Testament Apocrypha Book of Second Esdras (4:1–4), where he instructs Esdras (the Greek form of Ezra) "from whence the wicked heart cometh." Uriel also appears in the Book of Enoch, a pseudoepigraphic Jewish-Christian work, where he is the watcher over the world and the lowest part of hell. He serves as principal guide to Enoch in his various visions.

The angel Chamuel is identified in Jewish folklore as the angel who wrestled with Jacob (Genesis 32:24–32). In

Christian tradition Chamuel is the angel who comforted Jesus in the Garden of Gethsemane (Luke 22:43). Neither Biblical text gives the name of the angel.

Jewish folklore credits the next angel, Zophiel, with driving Adam and Eve from the Garden of Eden. The account in Genesis 3:23–24 nowhere mentions an angel, but "the Lord God" himself as responsible for casting out the couple. Milton in *Paradise Lost* (Book 6) calls Zophiel "of cherubim the swiftest wing."

The last of the seven, Zadkiel, is credited in both Jewish and Christian folklore with being the angel who held back the knife when Abraham was about to sacrifice his son Isaac (Genesis 22:1–18), though the angel's name is not given in the Biblical text. In another Jewish work, Zadkiel is credited with leading the Israelites out of Egypt.

Not included in the list of the seven, yet one of the most important angelic beings in Jewish folklore, is Sammael, the angel of death. He appears in many Jewish folktales as a dispenser of death, under the control of God's will.

One folktale tells how Sammael is outwitted by two clever foxes. Sammael asks God for permission to kill two of every creature, since as yet no one has died in the world and Sammael is perhaps growing restless. God grants the request with the proviso that nothing be killed before its allotted time. Sammael agrees and then proceeds to kill two of every creature. He comes upon two foxes and is about to murder them when they cry out that he has already killed their parents.

"Look into the water," they say to Sammael. The angel looks down, sees the reflection of the two foxes, and thinking that they are the bodies of two he has already killed, is fooled by the ruse—and leaves the foxes alone.

Longfellow's poetic drama *Christus: A Mystery* (1872) includes a scene in a village school in which the young Judas Iscariot, later the betrayer of Jesus, is being taught by a rabbi. The rabbi asks Judas why dogs howl at night. Judas replies that "dogs howl when the icy breath" of the "Great Sammael, the Angel of Death" is making his flight "through the town."

Sammael is described by the rabbi in Longfellow's poem as "full of eyes," and the young Judas adds that he holds a "sword, from which doth fall . . . a drop of gall" into the mouth of the dying.

There is yet another demonic creature, Yezer Hara ("Evil imagination," or "Evil inclination"), who figures prominently in Jewish Rabbinical works. The term *Yezer Hara* is believed to be derived from two Biblical texts, both in Genesis: "And God saw that the wickedness of man was great in the earth, and that every imagination (*yezer*) of the thoughts of his heart was only evil continually" (6:5); and "for the imagination (*yezer*) of man's heart is evil from his youth." (8:21) In time the rabbis added *hara* ("Evil"), creating a being responsible for man's sinful nature.

One rabbi, R. Simon ben Lakish, wrote, "Satan and Yezer and the Angel of Death are one." This sweeping statement takes into account all Evil. As many of the rabbis write about Yezer Hara, his role returns to that of Satan of the Old Testament, that of "adversary," since his main activity consists in seducing and tempting mankind. One Jewish folktale gives a case in point.

When the great patriarch Abraham was on his way to Mount Moriah to sacrifice his son Isaac, Satan (the identification of Satan with Yezer Hara is complete in this folktale) said to him, "Old man, where are you going?"

Abraham replied, "I am going to fulfill the will of my Father in Heaven."

"What did he tell you?" Satan asked.

"To bring my son to him as a burnt-offering," Abraham replied.

"That an old man like you should make such a mistake!"

replied Satan. "God only wanted to lead you astray. Isn't it written in the Scriptures 'Whoso sheddeth man's blood, by man shall his blood be shed'? (Genesis 9:6) If you sacrifice your son, you are a murderer."

Satan's intention, using Biblical quotation to his own advantage, is to tempt Abraham to go against God's order. Yet as all Jewish writings point out, Yezer Hara, Satan, and all angelic beings, Good or Evil, are the creations of the One True God and are under his control. They are not separate demonic beings arising from some cosmic struggle with a Good God.

We therefore return to the main theme in the Old Testament—the One, True, and Only God. In the book of Lamentations, ascribed to the prophet Jeremiah but possibly written by someone else, we have:

> Who has only to speak to make things exist?
>   Who commands, if not the Lord?
> From where, if not from the mouth of the Most High,
>   do evil and good come?

> (Lamentations 3:37–38, The Jerusalem Bible)

Chapter 5

Christian Mythology and Folklore

The conflict between the Kingdom of God and the Kingdom of the Devil appears in the New Testament, establishing a series of motifs which constantly appear in European folklore.

Three of the four Gospels in the New Testament record the Temptations of Jesus by the Devil (Mark 1:12–13; Matthew 4:1–11; Luke 4:1–13). The following account is based on Luke in the King James Version.

After his baptism, Jesus was moved by the Holy Spirit to go into the wilderness. For forty days he fasted and was tempted by the Devil. At the end of his fast the Devil said, "If thou be the Son of God, command this stone that it be made bread."

Jesus replied, "It is written, 'That man shall not live by bread alone, but by every word of God.' "

Then the Devil took Jesus to a high mountain and showed him all the kingdoms of the world.

"All this power will I give thee," the Devil said, "and the glory of them: for that is delivered unto me; and to whomsoever I will I give it. If thou therefore wilt worship me, all shall be thine."

Jesus answered, "Get thee behind me, Satan, for it is written, 'Thou shalt worship the Lord thy God, and him only shalt thou serve.' "

The Devil then took Jesus to Jerusalem and placed him on "a pinnacle of the temple."

"If thou be the Son of God," the Devil said, "cast thyself down from hence, for it is written,

"He shall give his angels charge over thee, to keep thee:
And in their hands they shall bear thee up, lest at any time
    thou dash thy foot against a stone."

Jesus said, "Thou shalt not tempt the Lord thy God."

When the Devil had finished all the temptations, "he departed from him for a season."

Jesus's Temptations by the Devil are to test whether Jesus's calling, which he received at his baptism, was genuine. Thus in the first temptation the Devil offers Jesus the opportunity to perform a miracle: turn a stone into bread to satisfy hunger. This act would immediately prove that Jesus first considered his physical need and not the preaching of the Kingdom of God. Jesus therefore rejects the Devil's interpretation of his Messiahship. In the second temptation the Devil offers Jesus an earthly kingdom, since the Devil is "the god of this world." (II Corinthians 4:4) Jesus again refuses, since he does not see his Messiahship as the establishment of an earthly kingdom which he will rule. The last temptation tests whether Jesus would tempt God to act by saving Jesus from falling from the "pinnacle of the temple." The Devil is asking Jesus to force God to perform a miracle. Jesus again refuses, since he does not see his Messiahship in this light, for he is God's servant, not ruler.

Who is this Devil that appears in all the narratives and is called Satan? Certainly he is not the Satan of the Old Testament, who was God's servant, being merely an "adversary" to man. Satan has become a demonic being of this world who opposes God's rule, which Jesus has come to establish. Some modern interpretations of the Temptations of Jesus see the entire action taking place in the mind of Jesus, with the Devil merely an illusion or personification, of Evil. This may be the truth for most of us today, though in Jesus's time the Devil was viewed as a corporeal figure, a demonic being who ruled the world and was the founder of an empire that constantly struggled with and counteracted the Kingdom of God. This belief is found in nonscriptural Jewish writings (though not in the Old Testament) and was inherited by Christianity.

Mark's Gospel, believed to be the earliest of the four, constantly makes reference to Jesus's encounters with the Kingdom of the Devil. The story of Jesus's first "sign" (the New Testament never uses the Greek word *thauma*, "miracle," but instead uses "sign" for Jesus's healing and other proofs of power) tells of a man who was possessed by an Evil spirit (Mark 1:23–28). Jesus was teaching in the synagogue when "a man with an unclean spirit" came in.

"Let us alone," the man cried. "What have we to do with thee, thou Jesus of Nazareth? Art thou come to destroy us? I know thee who thou art, the Holy One of God."

Jesus said, "Hold thy peace, and come out of him."

The Evil spirit then "cried with a loud voice" and came out of the man. The people asked in astonishment: "What is this? What new doctrine is this? For with authority commandeth he even the unclean spirits, and they do obey him."

Throughout Mark we have the Kingdom of the Devil retreating before Jesus. "And unclean spirits, when they saw him, fell down before him, and cried, saying, 'Thou art the Son of God.' " (Mark 3:11) Constantly Jesus instructs the demons not to tell anyone who he is. When he calls his disciples, Jesus tells them, "I will also send you out to preach, and you will have authority to drive out demons." (Mark 3:14–15, Good News Bible)

This power which Jesus promised his followers has been invoked by the Christian Church through the centuries in various rites of exorcism. For example, the Roman Rite of Baptism for centuries contained a ritual of exorcism. Here are some excerpts, as found in *The Daily Missal of the Mystical Body* edited by The Maryknoll Fathers and published in 1960:

Priest: I exorcise you, unclean spirit, in the name of the † Father, and of the † Son, and of the Holy † Spirit. Come out and leave this servant of God (*name*). Accursed and damned spirit, hear the command of God himself, he who walked upon the sea and extended his right hand to Peter as he was sinking. Therefore, accursed devil, acknowledge your condemnation; pay homage to the true and living God; pay homage to Jesus Christ, his Son, and to the Holy Spirit, and depart from this servant of God, (*name*), for Jesus Christ, our Lord and God, has called him/her to his holy grace and blessing, and to the font of Baptism.

The priest traces with his thumb on the forehead of the child the sign of the cross, the mark of the Christian.

Never dare, accursed devil, to violate the sign of the holy cross † which we place upon his/her forehead. Through Christ our Lord.

The present Roman Rite of Baptism has altered this prayer, though the Lord's Prayer, which is the basic Christian prayer, contains reference to being delivered from the Devil. In the Good News Bible, the last verse of the prayer is translated, "Do not bring us to hard testing, but keep us safe from the Evil One." The traditional translation, "deliver us from evil," still recited in most churches certainly misses the point of the prayer's petition, which is not about abstract Evil, but concrete Evil in the person of the Devil himself.

In Christianity the belief in the corporeal existence of the Devil assumed its greatest force during the Middle Ages. The great Roman Catholic Doctor of the Church Saint Thomas Aquinas believed in devils, witches, incubi, and succubi. When he wrote a commentary on the Biblical Book of Job, he identified the monster Behemoth as the Devil. Taking one verse in Job (40:16), which describes the monster:

> Lo now, his strength is in his loins,
> and his force is in the navel of his belly.

the Doctor then concluded that the Devil could have sexual intercourse with humans. When the Devil assumed a female form (a succubus), he seduced men. When he as-

sumed a male form (an incubus), he impregnated women.
The result of this sexual union produced, according to
Aquinas, a human being, though the child would be more
cunning than children of an ordinary human couple.

Aquinas's many explanations of Christian doctrine find
their full expression in the great poem of the late Middle
Ages *The Divine Comedy* by Dante. In this massive work
the entire universe is ordered according to Scholastic
teaching. The poem, divided into three sections, Hell,
Purgatory, and Heaven, contains many descriptions of
demons, and of course Satan. Dante described the three-
faced Satan (who is a parody of the Christian Trinity) in
the last canto of the Hell section:

> Oh, what a sight!
> How passing strange it seemed when I did spy
> Upon his head three faces: one in front
> Of hue vermilion, the other two with this
> Midway each shoulder joined and at the crest;
> The right 'twixt wan and yellow seemed; the left
> To look upon, such as comes from whence old Nile
> Stoops to the lowlands. Under each shot forth
> Two mighty wings, enormous as became
> A bird so vast. No plumes had they,
> But were in texture like a bat, and these
> He flapped in the air, that from him issued still
> Three winds wherewith Cocytus to its depth
> Was frozen. At six eyes he wept: the tears
> Adown three chins distilled with bloody foam.
> At every mouth his teeth a sinner champed,
> Bruised as with ponderous engine; so that three
> Were in this guise tormented.
>
> *(Cary translation)*

The three who are being chewed by Satan are Judas Iscariot, who betrayed Jesus, and Brutus and Cassius, who

betrayed Julius Caesar. Dante left out Pontius Pilate since, to placate the Roman Empire, Christianity forgave his part in the killing of Jesus. In fact one branch of the Eastern Church lists Pilate among the saints.

Dante's descriptions of hell, purgatory, and heaven were not his own devising but were based on a thousand years of Christian legend and tradition. In one early non-scriptural Christian work, Saint Peter is made to describe hell:

And I saw another place right opposite, rough and being the place of punishment. And those who are punished there and the punishing angels had their robes dark; as the color of the air of the place is also dark; and some people were hung up by their tongues: they were those who had blasphemed the path of righteousness; and underneath them a bright baneful fire was lit.

The description goes on considerably longer, but this excerpt shows the basis for the elaborate punishments meted out in Dante's hell. Another source which may have influenced Dante, since it also had its effects on Christian tradition, is found in the *Pistis Sophia*, a third-century work by Christian Gnostics. Gnosticism, which had many forms, taught the belief that there are two gods, one Good God (the father of Jesus) and one Evil one (the creator, who is the God of the Old Testament). This heresy also believed that the divine spark, the soul, had to escape from the body, since physical matter was Evil because it was controlled by Evil spirits. Only by *gnosis* ("knowledge") of the unknown god and the redeemer who comes to earth could one be saved, but this salvation was limited to only a few.

The *Pistis Sophia* reveals all the elaborate machinery of hell. In one of its sections Mary Magdalene asks Jesus to describe the various regions of hell. Jesus replies:

The outer darkness is a huge dragon, with its tail in its mouth; it is outside the world and surroundeth it completely. There are many regions of punishment therein, for there are in it twelve dungeons of horrible torment. In each dungeon there is a ruler.

These rulers are, according to the *Pistis Sophia,* various demons who are then named and given elaborate descriptions.

The elaborate machinery of hell passed on from Dante and these earlier sources found fertile ground during the Reformation, for even though the Reformers omitted purgatory from their doctrine, they accepted the Devil and all his works. The great Protestant Reformer Martin Luther, for example, firmly believed in devils, witches, succubi, and incubi, just as Saint Thomas Aquinas had.

Luther wrote that he was constantly annoyed by the Devil, who tried to stop his work, especially when he was translating the Bible into German. There is a legend that Luther once threw an inkstand at the fiend. Being on such familiar terms with the Devil, it is not strange to find Luther writing, "Early this morning when I awoke the fiend came and began disputing with me. 'Thou art a great sinner,' said he. I replied, 'Canst thou not tell me something new, Satan?' "

Luther, like Aquinas, believed in the Devil's power to assist wizards and witches in their Evil designs. Following Saint Augustine's authority, Luther had come to believe in incubi and succubi, since Satan in the form of a handsome man loves to decoy young girls. Luther also accepted belief in changelings, children of the Devil who replace human children.

Both Catholic and Protestant Christianity agreed on a belief in witches. The *Malleus Maleficarum* ("Witch Hammer"), a handbook on witchcraft written by two Dominicans and published in 1487, was used by Catholic and Protestant alike in the persecution of witches. It summed up the belief held by Christianity at the time: "The greatest heresy is not to believe in witchcraft."

Part of the machinery of witchcraft involved a compact with the Devil. Numerous legends of men or women who sold their souls to the Devil abound in European folklore. The best-known expression of this motif is found in the legend of Faust. It was originally a German tale written to protest the new humanism of the Reformation age, as many believed this humanism would lead to atheism. The German work appeared in English in 1582 as *The Historie of the Damnable Life, and Deserved Death of Doctor John Faustus*, translated from the German by "P.F."

In the book the aged scholar Faust makes a bargain with Mephistopheles (in Hebrew, "he who loves not the light") to give the Devil his soul at death in exchange for an immediate return of his youth. The theme of Faust appealed to the English writer Christopher Marlowe, whose play *The Tragical History of Doctor Faustus* (1593) uses some elements from the book. In the play, Mephistopheles is the leading demonic character. When Faustus asks how he is "out of hell," the demon replies:

> Why, this is Hell, nor am I out of it:
> Thinkest thou that I, who saw the face of God,
> and tasted th'eternal joys of heaven,
> Am not tormented with ten thousand hells,
> In being depriv'd of everlasting bliss?

For this speech to be fully understood, one must be aware that Marlowe assumed his audience would recall the legend of the Fall of the Angels, which Christianity had evolved from various scriptural and nonscriptural sources. The one that first comes to mind is found in II Peter 2:4:

"God spared not the angels that sinned, but cast them down to Hell, and delivered them into chains of darkness, to be reserved unto the judgment." This short verse sums up the Christian myth accounting for the origin of devils. They are angels who revolted against God.

A second verse supporting the myth is found in Luke 10:18: "I beheld Satan as lightning fall from heaven." This quotation in turn recalls a verse in the Old Testament, Isaiah 14:12: "How art thou fallen from heaven, O Lucifer, son of the morning." Saint Jerome, the translator of the Latin Vulgate, equated Lucifer in the Old Testament with Satan in the New when he translated the Bible. This interpretation was then accepted by the Early Church. Later Dante in *The Divine Comedy* made Lucifer the king of hell, and Milton in *Paradise Lost* applied the name Lucifer to Satan before the Fall.

The legend of the Fall of the Angels is beautifully told in an Anglo-Saxon poem, *Genesis*, ascribed to Caedmon (*fl.* 670 A.D.):

> The Almighty had disposed ten angel-tribes,
> The holy Father by His strength of hand,
> That they whom He well trusted should serve Him
> And work His will. For that the holy God
> Gave intellect, and shaped them with His hands.
> In happiness He placed them, and to one
> He added prevalence and might of thought,
> Sway over much, next highest to Himself
> In heaven's realm. Him He had wrought so bright
> That pure as starlight was in heaven the form
> Which God the Lord of hosts had given him.
> Praise to the Lord his work, and cherishing
> Of heavenly joy, and thankfulness to God
> For his share of that gift of light, which then
> Had long been his. But he perverted it,
> Against heaven's highest Lord he lifted war,

Against the Most High in His sanctuary. . . .
He raised himself against his Maker, sought
Speech full of hate and bold presuming boast,
Refused God suit, said that his own form beamed
With radiance of light, shone bright of hue,
And in his mind he found not service due
To the Lord God, for to himself he seemed
In force and skill greater than all God's host
. . . God, then cast him down
To the deep dale of hell, where he became
Devil. The fiend with all his comrades fell
From heaven, angels, for three nights and days,
From heaven to hell, where the Lord changed them all
To devils.

Christianity supplies the myth for the origin of Satan and his devils, and it also provides them a proper end. In Revelation, that mysterious and strange book that closes the New Testament, there is a description of the end of time. John writes:

And there was a war in heaven: Michael and his angels fought against the dragon; and the dragon fought and his angels, and prevailed not; neither was their place found any more in heaven. And the great dragon was cast out, that old serpent, called the Devil, and Satan, which deceiveth the whole world: he was cast out into the earth, and his angels were cast out with him. (12:7–9)

Satan will be bound for a thousand years. Then he will be set loose, appearing with anti-Christ, a figure who will deceive men. Throughout history various Evil persons have been assigned the role of anti-Christ: Caligula, Simon Magus, Nero, Napoleon, Hitler, and Stalin among them. During the Reformation the Pope was often cited by Protestants as anti-Christ. When the reign of anti-Christ comes to an end, Satan and his crew will be "cast into a lake of fire and brimstone . . . and shall be tormented day and night forever and ever." (Revelation 20:10) A new heaven and a new earth will arise, and a New Jerusalem, "And God shall wipe away all tears from their eyes; and there shall be no more death, neither sorrow, nor crying, neither shall there be any more pain: for the former things are passed away." (21:4)

Chapter 6

Armenian Mythology and Folklore

The demonic and beneficent spirits in ancient Armenian mythology were converted to Christian uses when the nation embraced the new faith.

The conversion of Armenia to Christianity, said to have taken place when Saint Gregory the Illuminator baptized King Tiridates III (AD 238–314), made Armenia the first nation to embrace Christianity officially. With the coming of the new religion, the ancient pagan myths and legends had either to be dismissed as lies or adjusted to the new beliefs. In Armenia as in other places, as Christianity spread, the latter course was followed. This tactic was a most common Christian approach to paganism. Instead of denying the existence of the ancient gods, the Church merely said they were demons who had come to lead people astray from the true God. Now that Christ had come, the demons no longer should be worshiped.

Since some pagan gods had beneficent aspects, the Church took those aspects and applied them to its own saints. Thus the attributes of Vahagan, the Armenian god of the sun, lightning, and fire, who was noted for his hunting abilities, were transferred to Athenogenes, a bishop and martyr of the early fourth century (feast, July 16), who was invoked as the patron saint of game and hunting. Vahagan had in the earlier mythology also been associated with the sea. He reappeared in Armenian folklore as Dsovean ("sea born") but was now accompanied by his wife Dsovinar, an angry storm-spirit.

The most notable examples of the Christian transference of pagan gods to its own uses are found in the Armenian translation of the Bible. The translators used the ancient, well-known spirits from the mythological past to make the Biblical message meaningful to their readers. The Jewish Passover, for example, is called the Festival of Zatik, in honor of the ancient god Zatik, who is believed by most modern scholars to have been a god of vegetation. Zatik was worshiped at a spring festival about the time of Easter. To this day Easter is still called the Festival of Zatik by Armenian Christians.

When Isaiah 13:21 was translated into Armenian, two ancient demonic spirits appeared in the text. Here is the passage in the King James Version:

> But wild beasts of the desert shall lie there;
> And their houses shall be full of doleful creatures;
> And owls shall dwell there,
> And satyrs shall dance there.

The Armenian version substitutes *Hambarus* for "owls" and *Devs* for "satyrs." In earlier Armenian mythology both the Hambarus and the Devs were demonic spirits who lived in desert places, often assuming grotesque human or animal forms. Their demonic natures varied somewhat, depending on the situation. In the national epic poem of Armenia, *David of Sassoun*, they appear in an Evil light.

One day, the epic tells, Hambarus and Devs stole some calves that were being guarded by David. The hero followed the tracks they left and came to the entrance to a cave. He paused for a moment, then cried out with such a loud voice that the Devs inside became "so full of fear as is the Devil when Christ's voice is heard in Hell."

Not wishing to have a fight, the Devs' leader told his monster-men to go outside to greet David before the hero came into the cave and killed them all. The Devs went out one by one, and David struck them with an oak cudgel. Their heads rolled off onto the ground where David cut off their ears. He then killed their leader and took the treasure that was hidden in the cave.

This short episode illustrates how the Judeo-Christian hero David is given Christlike qualities: His voice instills fear, as when Christ made his descent into hell to free the ancient spirits held captive by the Devil.

Christ's descent into hell, which forms part of the Christian Creed ("He descended into hell") is the parallel of an ancient mythological motif of the hero descending to the nether regions. Other examples are those of Odysseus in *The Odyssey* and Aeneas in *The Aeneid*. In one ancient Christian account found in *The Gospel of Nicodemus*, we have Satan, called "the prince and captain of death," say to the prince of hell: "Prepare to receive Jesus of Nazareth himself, who boasted he was the Son of God, and yet was a man afraid of death." Then there is a loud sound of thunder, and a voice crying out, "Lift up your gates, O Princes; and be ye lifted up, ye gates of Hell, and the King of Glory shall come in." The Lord appears "in the form of a man, and lightened those places which had ever before been in darkness, and broke asunder the fetters which before could not be broken; and with his invincible power visited those who sat in the deep darkness of iniquity, and the shadow of death by sin."

At Christ's approach, the demons "were seized with . . . horror, and with the most submissive fear." Christ tramples upon Death and seizes the prince of hell, depriving him of all his power. He stretches forth his hand, saying, "Come to me, all ye saints, who are created in my image, who were condemned by the tree of the forbidden fruit, and by the devil and death; live now by the word of my cross; the devil, the prince of the world, is overcome, and death is conquered."

Though death and the Devil are said to have been conquered, both constantly reappear in Christian Armenian folklore accompanied by a host of demonic spirits. Thus the Armenian Church, using the pagan past, calls Salome, who danced to obtain the head of Saint John the Baptist, "more bloodthirsty than the Nhangs of the Sea." Nhangs were demonic spirits who sucked blood, vampirelike, from their victims. The Virgin Mary is called "Hayk-like" by Saint Gregory of Narek, recalling an ancient Armenian hero, Hayk, who freed his people from the bondage of

King Bel. The name is applied to the Virgin because she bore Christ, who freed his people from the bondage of the Devil.

Christ himself is identified with Shahapet, a beneficent serpent-spirit who inhabited olive trees and vinestocks in the ancient mythology. One Armenian Christian writer of the third century calls Christ the "Shahapet of the grave-yards." At first this image may seem strange and out of place, but it is actually a very clever use of the pagan past, and in accordance with Biblical imagery. The Old Testament gives the image of the brazen serpent (Numbers 21:8–9) which was erected by Moses to save the people. Those who looked upon the serpent hung on a crosslike beam were saved from plague. In the New Testament (John 3:14–15), recalling the saving image of the serpent, Jesus said of himself, "And as Moses lifted up the serpent in the wilderness, even so must the Son of Man be lifted up." This of course refers to Christ's Crucifixion and Resurrection.

Less elevated than the image of Shahapet is that of the Javersaharses and Kaches, spirits in Armenian folklore who preside over marriage and childbirth. They love to attend weddings and will be helpful if they like you, but if not, they will become angry and cause trouble. Both are often cited by Armenian Christian writers as Evil spirits, since the wicked Armenian King Edward built a temple to worship the Kaches.

One spirit, the Al, is a fitting end to this list, since he combines Persian, Persian-Islamic, and Armenian-Christian imagery and is found in all three mythologies. Als are half-human, half-animal, of both sexes, and live in watery, damp, and sandy places. One Armenian Christian legend tells of an encounter between Saint Peter and Saint Paul and an Al.

One day Saint Peter and Saint Paul were traveling and

came to a man who was sitting in the sand by a roadside. His hair was made of snakes, his eyebrows of brass, his eyes of glass, his face was as white as snow, his teeth were made of iron, and he had a tusk like a wild boar.

"What are you? You ugly, unclean beast," the saints said to him.

"I am the wicked Al. I sit upon the child-bearing mother, I scorch her ears and pull out her liver. I strangle both mother and child. Our food is the flesh of little children. We steal unborn infants of eight months and bring them to our demon-king. The abyss, the corners of houses, and stables are our abode."

To prevent the Al from doing his Evil work, sabers and other weapons are placed under a woman's pillow. After a child is born, the woman is kept awake so the Als do not have the opportunity to catch her sleeping.

Armenian folklore, with its combination of ancient mythology and Christianity, does not offer a new solution to the problem of Good and Evil. It illustrates well the adaptation of the past to present uses. The demonic spirits were a reality for the pagans as well as for the Armenian Christians.

Chapter 7

Islamic Mythology and Folklore

Allah, the One, True, and Only God, and his creation, Iblis, the Devil, act out the eternal conflict between Good and Evil.

When Allah was forming man, he took clay and, after shaping it, left it to dry for some forty days or forty years. (There are variant accounts of the myth.) All the *malaika* (angels who were created from rays of light) came to see Allah's new work. Among them was Iblis ("despair"), one of Allah's most important angels. Iblis looked at the new creation, and knowing that Allah intended to make Adam more important than any angel, he kicked the clay with his foot until it resounded throughout the heavens and earth. Allah then called all the angels to come and honor Adam. Iblis refused because, as the Koran (Sura 2), phrases it, Iblis "was puffed up with pride." This description makes Iblis fit neatly in with the Christian concept of a Satan who fell from grace because of his pride.

In anger Allah said Iblis was to be cast out of heaven, but Iblis called out to Allah, "Grant me time. Do not banish me to outer darkness yet. Let me tempt Adam and his sons and see if he is worthy of your gifts and honor. Then we will see if he has Faith."

"I will grant your wish," replied Allah, "until the Day of Judgment. When that Day comes you will regret your evil deeds and pay dearly for them. You will be cast into a dark pit, never again to harm any souls. Now leave heaven."

The test proposed to Allah by Iblis recalls Satan's proposal to God in the Book of Job in the Old Testament, and Iblis's final punishment recalls the last days of Satan described in the Book of Revelation in the New Testament, when he will be finally bound in a bottomless pit. We must remember that Iblis, similar to the case of Satan, cannot act unless the supreme one god Allah grants him permission. There is no equality between Allah and Iblis. The supreme ruler is God; he allows or permits the presence of Evil.

In his Evil work, Iblis is aided by a host of offspring called *djinn*, or *genii*. These spirits of "subtle fire" are believed by most scholars to be descended from nature demons who lived in unclean or deserted places. They were absorbed into Islamic mythology, as were many other demons and spirits from the pagan Arabs.

Djinn are divided into different categories, though Islamic folklore is not always clear in its distinctions, many names being just different words for a demonic being. The orders are: jann, the lowest and weakest; the djinn proper, who often appear in animal form; the shaitans, or sayatins; and ifrits. In all there are some forty troops of 6,000,000 djinn according to one count.

When King Solomon, who often appears in Islamic legend, first saw the djinn he was horrified at how ugly they were. He used his magic ring to gain mastery over them, forcing some to help him build his great temple. A modern Islamic folktale tells of a family so tormented by djinn, which appeared in various animal shapes, that the family went into the desert, the home of the djinn, and killed all the animals they could capture. This so reduced the population of djinn that Allah (who wanted to maintain a balance in his order of nature) had to intervene and a truce was made to ensure that the djinn would not be wiped out entirely.

The Koran (Sura 6) tells how the djinn believed "in their ignorance" that Allah had "sons and daughters." Some djinn were converted by Muhammad to Islam and are diligent followers of the rites. They often appear as "household serpents" who protect the family, much in the manner of *genii* in Roman mythology.

In Morocco djinn are called jnun and often appear in toad form. If they do, they are politely asked to leave the house since their presence often upsets the family.

The shaitans are a more dangerous breed of djinn than

the djinn proper. Allah created al-Shaitan (perhaps another name for Iblis), who then produced eggs from which
other demons were hatched. In a variant myth, Allah
created not only al-Shaitan but a wife, who then produced
three eggs containing their offspring. The children were
all ugly, having hoofed feet. Shaitans are even more ugly
in their eating habits. They like excrement and other dirt
and waste, and prefer the shade to sunlight. It is believed
that every man has a shaitan or personal demon, just as he
does a guardian angel. Sometimes the shaitan is considered
the muse of inspiration in poets.

Ifrits are an even more dangerous collection than shaitans. Originally the word may have meant one who over-
comes an antagonist and rolls him in the dust. In time the
term was applied to a very powerful and always malicious
djinn. The Koran (Sura 27) makes a brief mention of a
spirit as "an ifrit, one of the djinn." Islamic legend has
added details to this brief Koranic description. In Egypt
the word has come to mean the ghost of a murdered man
or one who has died a violent death. Yet the female version of the ifrit, the ifriteh, which is mentioned in the
Thousand and One Nights, is a benevolent djinn. In fact in
"The Second Old Man's Story," a pious woman is turned
into an ifriteh and carries the hero to an island to save his
life. In the morning she returns and says to him, "I have
paid thee my debt, for it is I who bore thee up out of the
sea and saved thee from death, by permission of Allah.
Know that I am of the djinn who believe in Allah and
his Prophet."

While as the father of the djinn, Iblis is the best-known
Fallen Angel in Islam, he has two very important broth-
ers: Harut and Marut. According to the Koran (Sura 102),
Harut and Marut teach men "how to cause division be-
tween man and wife." However, the two can work their
Evil only by the permission of Allah. A number of legends

are connected with the passage in the Koran. In one account, when the angels saw how sinful men were, they spoke contemptuously of them to Allah.

"If you were in their place," Allah replied, "you would do no better."

The angels did not agree with Allah, and two, Harut and Marut, were chosen for an experiment to test the truth of the matter. They flew down to earth from heaven. Allah told them that they were to abstain from idolatry, whoredom, murder, and the drinking of wine (these are forbidden to a good Muslim). When the two came upon a beautiful woman, Zorba (or Zurah), they fell victim to her sexual charms. They were discovered in the act by a man whom they killed, hoping no one would learn of their deed.

Allah, looking down from heaven, saw all that happened. The angels were called to see what Harut and Marut had committed. "In truth, Thou wast right," they replied to Allah.

Harut and Marut were then given the choice of suffering in this world or the next. Cleverly they chose to suffer on earth. They were thrown into a "well in the town of Babylon where, loaded with chains," they took up the business of teaching men magic and sorcery. (In Persian the word *harut* is used for a magician.)

If the two Fallen Angels had chosen Jahannam, or hell, they would have met Malec, the principal angel in charge of hell. He is the ruler of the Zabaniya, the guardians of hell according to one interpretation of their role, or in another reading, angels who carry the souls after death.

The plight of the wicked is vividly described in the Koran (Sura 43) when they call upon Malec to "intercede" for them with Allah. The angel remains silent and will answer the sinners a thousand years after the Day of Judgment. When he does, however, he will offer little hope, for he will say they will remain there to suffer forever.

Those unlucky enough to be in hell are there because they did not pass their examination in the Faith by Munkar and Nakir. These two angels command the dead to sit upright in their tombs when they are to be tested in the Faith. Both the faithful and sinners are questioned. If the correct answer is given, that Muhammad is the Prophet or Apostle of Allah, the body will receive air from paradise. If no answer or an incorrect one is given, the sinner is beaten. After the beating, the sinner feels the pressure of the earth against his body as his tomb is invaded by dragonlike beasts that gnaw at him until the Day of Resurrection, when all mankind will appear before Allah.

All men are called by the angel of death, Azrael (or Izrael). He keeps a roll containing the name of every person born in the world. The time of death and whether the person is saved or damned is not known to Azrael. When the day of a person's death approaches, Allah lets a leaf with the name written upon it fall from below his majestic throne. Azrael reads the name and within forty days must separate the soul from the body. If the person causes a struggle, Azrael flies back to the throne of Allah and informs him. Allah gives Azrael an apple from paradise on which the *basmala,* or Name of God, "the merciful and compassionate," is written. When the person reads the Name of God, he then gives up his life to the angel of death.

If, however, the person is an unbeliever and is lost, Azrael roughly tears the soul from the body. The gate of heaven closes and the person is cast into hell.

Azrael is variously described in Islamic writings. In general he has some 70,000 feet and 4,000 wings. His body has four faces and many eyes and tongues.

Henry Wadsworth Longfellow, in one of his metrical poems included in *Tales of a Wayside Inn* (1863), has the

Spanish Jew tell a tale of Azrael and King Solomon. The king is entertaining a "learned man" who is a rahjah. As they walk, the guest sees a white figure in the twilight air gazing intently at him. The man asks Solomon:

> What is yon shape, that, pallid as the dead,
> Is watching me, as if he sought to trace
> In the dim light the features of my face?

The king rather calmly tells his guest that it is Azrael, the angel of death. The man begs King Solomon to get him as far away from Azrael as possible. The king, with his magic ring, sends him off to India. The angel of death then asks King Solomon who the man was that left so suddenly, and the king gives the man's name. Azrael thanks the king for sending the man to India, since he was on his way "to see him there."

Although Azrael announces the individual's death, Israfel will announce the end of the world. Israfel is not named directly in the Koran, but Islamic tradition has supplied the lack. He is considered an archangel. For three years he was the companion of Muhammad and trained him to be the Prophet. Gabriel, who in Islam is called Jiburili, then took over the task and dictated the Koran to the Prophet from its perfect copy in heaven.

Alexander the Great, another important figure in Islamic legend, met Israfel before he arrived in the Land of Darkness. There the angel stood upon a hill and blew the trumpet. Israfel's trumpet will announce the Day of Resurrection, when he will stand upon the Holy Rock in Jerusalem and give the signal which will bring the dead back to life and divide the Good from the Evil.

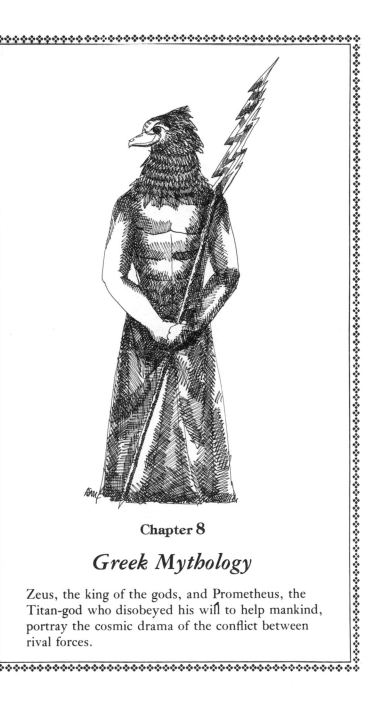

Chapter 8

Greek Mythology

Zeus, the king of the gods, and Prometheus, the Titan-god who disobeyed his will to help mankind, portray the cosmic drama of the conflict between rival forces.

After the gods defeated the Titans in the battle over who was to rule the world, the gods were negotiating with man about the honor to be paid to them. Since Prometheus ("Forethought") had helped Zeus defeat the Titan's brother giants, he was chosen to decide how sacrificial victims were to be offered to the gods. Prometheus cut up an ox and divided it into two parts. He wrapped the choice meat cuts in the skin of the ox and placed the stomach (which is not edible) on top of it to make it look unappetizing. The second part of the animal, which was made up of bones, Prometheus covered with fat to make it look desirable. Zeus had to make the choice of which portion was to be set aside for the gods. Zeus knew that Prometheus had set up a trick, but still Zeus chose the heap of bones and fat. As a punishment to mankind, however, Zeus deprived them of the gift of fire, leaving them in darkness and cold.

This move on the part of Zeus did not stop Prometheus, who, according to the Greek poet Hesiod in his *Theogony*, "cheated him, and stole the farseen splendor of untiring fire in a hollow fennelstalk" and gave it to man. (This grand gesture is captured in the famous statue of Prometheus in the skating rink at Rockefeller Center in New York City. It is somewhat ironic that the Rockefeller family, a symbol of the Establishment, should choose Prometheus, a symbol of Revolution, as the central figure to bedeck this major complex of capitalist business.)

Zeus, angered that man now had fire, called upon the smith-god, Hephaestus, to make of clay a beautiful woman, whom he called Pandora. Up to that time man had lived alone. Zeus called upon the goddess Athena, who "girded and arrayed Pandora in silver-white raiment" and "placed around her head lovely garlands freshbudding with meadow-flowers."

Hermes, the messenger of the gods, then carried to Pandora a jar or box as her dowry. In the jar was every Evil that was to come into the world. Pandora was brought before Epimetheus ("Afterthought"), the brother of Prometheus. Though Prometheus had warned his brother not to accept any gift from Zeus, Epimetheus was so moved by Pandora's beauty that he married her. Pandora removed the lid from the jar and out flew all the Evils, troubles, and diseases which until that time were unknown to mankind. Only Hope remained in the jar before Pandora closed it again. The misogynist Hesiod wrote, "Just so to mortal men high-thundering Zeus gave woman as an evil." The Christian Doctors of the Church in the early centuries echoed Hesiod, and instead of Pandora they used Eve as the focus of their diatribe against women.

Zeus was not satisfied with punishing mankind. He now turned to his enemy, Prometheus. The Titan was bound in adamantine chains to a pillar with an eagle (the Greek stories vary, some say vulture) who ate Prometheus's liver each day. The liver was restored again at night, only to be eaten again.

It is at this point in the myth that the drama by Aeschylus, *Prometheus Bound*, opens. Although Aeschylus wrote three plays (*Prometheus the Firebringer*, *Prometheus Bound*, and *Prometheus Released*), we have today only the second part of the trilogy.

In *Prometheus Bound* the Titan, still the opponent of Zeus, is portrayed as full of the most devoted love for mankind, making Prometheus a savior-type figure, similar to Osiris in Egyptian mythology. Aeschylus makes Prometheus the son of Themis, by whom he was put in possession of all the secrets of the future. In the war with the Titans Prometheus's advice assisted Zeus to final victory. But when Zeus, after the partition of the world, resolved

to destroy humanity and create a new race of beings in
their stead, Prometheus alone of all the gods (for he is also
a god, though of an older race than Zeus) was concerned
for the fate of mankind. Aeschylus therefore prefers to
reject the idea of Prometheus as a Trickster who deceives
Zeus, in contrast to Hesiod's portrayal of Prometheus's
character.

According to Aeschylus, Prometheus steals fire from
heaven to save mankind, giving people a chance to advance
civilization. At the beginning of the play Prometheus is
nailed to a mountain peak by Hephaestus as punishment
for this crime. (In one account of the myth, Zeus, not
wishing to admit that Prometheus is being punished for
bringing fire to man, circulates the lie that he is being
punished for trying to sleep with Athena, who invited him
to Olympus for a love affair. Sexual slander is at least as
ancient as the Greeks.)

Prometheus is visited on the rock by the daughters of
Oceanus, who sympathize with him, and by their father,
who advises Prometheus to submit to Zeus.

All the standard arguments for submitting to a greater
authority are given, and the right or wrong of the situation
is never broached by Oceanus.

After Prometheus refuses to yield, Io, another victim of
Zeus, enters. She has been transformed into a heifer and is
being driven from land to land by the jealousy of Hera,
the wife of Zeus, for having been loved by the god. (As
powerful as Zeus is, there is always something of the hen-
pecked husband about him in many of the myths.) Prometheus tells Io that she shall be restored to her shape and
bear a son, the father of a royal race, one of whom, Hercules, shall free Prometheus from his chains. Moreover
Prometheus prophesies that Zeus shall have a son who will
then dethrone his father. When Zeus hears of this, he
sends his lackey Hermes to demand the particulars of this

coming disaster. Prometheus defiantly refuses to reveal what he knows. In punishment Zeus cleaves the rock with his thunderbolts, and Prometheus sinks beneath the earth.

So ends *Prometheus Bound,* the second part of Aeschylus's trilogy. But the question remains: How was the conflict between Zeus and Prometheus to be resolved? Aeschylus's answer, in the third play, has been lost. The English Romantic poet Shelley wrote a lyrical drama, *Prometheus Unbound* (1819), in which he attempts to complete Aeschylus's cycle.

When Shelley's drama opens, Prometheus has been chained to the rock for ages, attended and comforted by the Oceanids Panthea and Ione (Shelley uses the Latin spellings for some of the Greek names). With the passing years Prometheus's hostility to Zeus has become less bitter, though the hero is still strong-willed and determined. He cannot remember, however, what curse he placed upon Zeus (Jupiter in the poem) until a phantom of Zeus, raised by Earth, the mother of Prometheus in Shelley's scheme, appears. Prometheus says he would gladly recall the curse, but he knows that Zeus will nevertheless be dethroned. In a last effort to learn the secret, Zeus sends down Hermes and the Furies, threatening Prometheus with more torture. Zeus the tyrant always resorts to more and more torture. On his refusal the Furies tell Prometheus of all the suffering Zeus is subjecting mankind to because of his actions. Panthea and Ione comfort Prometheus, then leave to reassure their sister Asia, whom Prometheus loves, in her retreat in the Indian Caucasus.

Meanwhile the day of Prometheus's freedom has arrived. Voices summon Asia down to the abode of Demogorgon (a personification which typifies for Shelley the all-pervading soul of all things). Asia learns of the coming liberation of Prometheus, and she ascends in one of the chariots of the Hours to witness his deliverance.

Zeus has just wedded Thetis. Demogorgon ascends to
Olympus, becomes incarnate in the child that is in Thetis,
and casts Zeus from the battlements of heaven. Prometheus is then freed from the rock by the hero Hercules
and reunited with Asia. The work ends with some of the
most majestic lines ever penned:

> To suffer woes which Hope thinks infinite;
> To forgive wrongs darker than death or night;
> To defy Power, which seems omnipotent;
> To love, and bear; to hope till Hope creates
> From its own wreck the thing it contemplates;
> Neither to change, nor falter, nor repent;
> This, like thy glory, Titan, is to be
> Good, great and joyous, beautiful and free;
> This is alone Life, Joy, Empire, and Victory?

In a preface to *Prometheus Unbound* (1819), Shelley gives
an interesting parallel between Prometheus and Satan:

The only imaginary being resembling in any degree Prometheus
is Satan; and Prometheus is, in my judgment, a more poetical
character than Satan, because, in addition to courage and majesty and firm and patient opposition to omnipotent force, he is
susceptible of being described as exempt from the taints of ambition, envy, revenge, and a desire for personal aggrandisement,
which in the Hero of *Paradise Lost*, interferes with the interest.
. . . Prometheus is, as it were, the type of the highest perfection of moral and intellectual nature, impelled by the purest and
the truest motives to the best and the noblest ends.

Although Shelley could think only of Satan, we can cite
the Early Doctors of the Christian Church, such as Tertullian, who called Christ *verus Prometheus* ("true Prometheus"), since he freed man from sin. The Passion of Christ
was compared to the passion suffered by Prometheus. In
both examples, the Greek and the Christian, it is a father-
figure who is responsible for the punishment.

So far we have discussed the conflict between Zeus and Prometheus as a cosmic struggle between the forces of oppression and freedom, yet another important myth is attached to Prometheus in Ovid's *Metamorphoses* (Book 1) in which Prometheus is made the actual creator of humankind:

> . . . Prometheus temper'd into paste,
> And, mixt with living streams, the godlike image cast.

> (*John Dryden translation*)

Goethe, another freedom-loving poet, took the image of Prometheus as the creator of man and combined it with a defiance against Zeus. In his poem *Prometheus* (which both Franz Schubert and Hugo Wolf set to music), the hero tells Zeus:

> Here sit I, forming mortals
> After my image;
> A race resembling me,
> To suffer, to weep,
> To enjoy, to be glad,
> And thee to scorn,
> As I.

The combination of defiance of omnipresent authority and the godly powers of creation have made Prometheus one of the most popular subjects in Western art. In addition to the works mentioned already, there are poems by Lord Byron, Henry Wadsworth Longfellow, Robert Bridges, James Russell Lowell, and Robert Graves, and paintings by Piero di Cosimo and Peter Paul Rubens. Musically Prometheus was an inspiration to Beethoven, the arch-Romantic revolutionary, in his ballet *Die Geschöpfe des Prometheus* ("The Creatures of Prometheus," 1801); the Russian "mystical" composer Alexander Scriabin in his

Prometheus, Poem of Fire for orchestra; and Franz Liszt in his symphonic poem *Prometheus* (1850). Liszt's work was written to celebrate the unveiling of a memorial statue in Weimar to Johann Gottfried von Herder, Romantic poet, essayist, and folklorist, who had written a poetical drama, *Prometheus.*

"From among his [Herder's] cantatas and poems in dramatic form," wrote Liszt in his preface to the score, "we agreed that his work based on the Prometheus myth best represented the views of the man who was called the 'Apostle of Humanity.' . . . The Prometheus myth is filled with mysterious ideas, dark traditions . . . filled with hope and despair. . . . Suffering and transfiguration (or apotheosis); that constitutes the central idea of the myth."

This excessively Romantic approach to the subject of Prometheus is offset by André Gide's masochistic view of the subject in the work *Le Prométhée Mal Enchaîné.* In Gide's treatment the eagle or vulture which daily feeds upon Prometheus's liver is being kept as a pet!

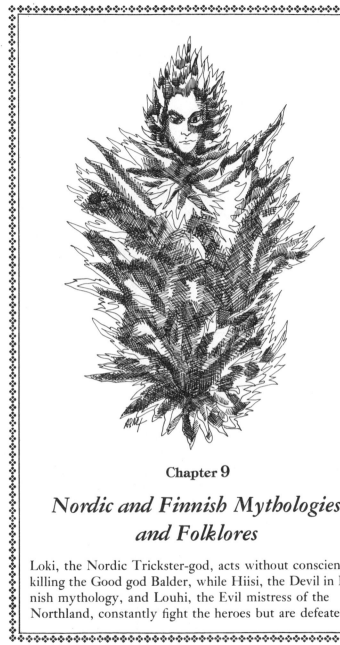

Chapter 9

Nordic and Finnish Mythologies and Folklores

Loki, the Nordic Trickster-god, acts without conscience, killing the Good god Balder, while Hiisi, the Devil in Finnish mythology, and Louhi, the Evil mistress of the Northland, constantly fight the heroes but are defeated.

A medieval Christian baptismal rite used in northern countries contained the following recitation by priest and candidate:

Q. Forsaketh thou the Devil?
A. I forsake the Devil!
Q. And all the Devil guilds?
A. And all Devil guilds.
Q. And all Devil works?
A. And I forsake all Devil works, and words, Thor and Woden (Odin) . . . and all the evil ones that are his companions.

This formula took into account the worship of the Nordic gods as an actuality. Therefore, instead of denying their existence, the Christian rite transformed them into demons, followers of the Devil. Christ and the saints then replaced these gods, Christ becoming a successor of the warrior-king Thor. Woden, father of Thor, was transformed into God the Father, while Christ's followers became his faithful vassals. Many pagan festivals were also adapted to the Christian liturgy to further complete the transformation. Yuletide became Christmas; Eastre, in honor of the goddess of spring, became Easter, giving us the name which became the English word.

Thor and Woden were identified as followers of the Devil, as his boon companions. The Devil himself was identified with an ancient Nordic god, Loki, who in many ways seems a parody of the gods Thor and Odin, just as the Devil is a parody of the Christian God. Loki was a Trickster, a creature in mythology and folklore who acts on impulse without regard to moral laws. Thus he is a being without conscience, an ambivalent mischief-maker, who corresponds to our modern folklore figures of Bugs Bunny in cartoons or to Br'er Rabbit in African and black American folklore. The difference, however, is that Loki went on to become almost completely identified with Evil in northern myth.

By the time the *Prose Edda*, a collection written by Snorri Sturluson of the myths of Nordic gods, was produced in the thirteenth century, Loki is called "the calumniator of the gods, the contriver of all fraud and mischief, and the disgrace of gods and men. . . . Many of the times he had exposed the gods to very great perils, and often extricated them again by his artifices."

One episode from the *Prose Edda* perfectly illustrates Loki in his role as Trickster. The myth concerns the building of a fortress by the gods to protect themselves from the giants who were always attempting to overthrow them. Even though Loki was of the giants' race, as was Prometheus in Greek myth, he said he would help the gods in their endeavor. While the gods were planning how the work was to be done, an unknown architect appeared among them and offered to undertake the construction provided the gods would give him the sun and moon and Freya, goddess of youth and beauty, as rewards. The gods at first objected, but Loki told them to accept the offer, promising he would devise a way to avoid payment. The gods agreed to pay the architect provided the fortress was finished in the course of a single winter. Another stipulation was that the architect was to use no help except for his horse, Svadilfare.

The unknown architect submitted to these conditions. Immediately he began work, hauling ponderous blocks of stone by night, building during the day. He progressed at such a rate that in a short time half of the project was completed. Near the end of winter, only one portion of the building remained to be finished.

Terrified that they would have to pay the architect his price, the gods went to Loki and said they would murder him unless he kept the architect from finishing the work on time. Changing himself into a mare (animal transformation is a common Trickster's feat in folklore), Loki rushed out of the forest. He neighed invitingly as the horse Svadilfare passed by dragging one of the great blocks of stone needed to finish the work. In a short time lust conquered the horse, and it ran off after the mare, closely followed by its angry master. Loki, as the mare, lured the two deep into the forest. Night was nearly gone and the work would now be impossible to finish. To complete his deceit, Loki had intercourse with the horse, later giving birth to Sleipner, an eight-footed horse used by the god Odin as his mount. Angry at the deceit, the architect returned to Asgard, the home of the gods, demanding payment, but Thor killed him with his magic hammer, Mjolnir.

When the gods realized that they had achieved their goal of the fortress through the use of deceit and murder, they knew their destruction was at hand. The important aspect of Nordic mythology is that it recognizes a moral order which even the gods themselves cannot maintain. This fact brings about their destruction, as they have failed to maintain the moral code for which they are responsible. The end of the gods was finally brought about by Loki's last crime, his murder of the Good god Balder.

One night Balder had a dream that he was to be murdered and told the gods of his sinister vision. The goddess Frigga, to forestall the disaster, went about to all created things—fire, water, iron, metals, stones, diseases, beasts, poisons, birds, serpents, and so on—exacting from them a promise that they would not injure Balder. All agreed. Time passed and the dream was forgotten. Because Balder remained invulnerable under the oath, it became a pastime for the gods to throw darts at him for amusement.

Loki of course had not forgotten his desire to kill the Good god. Disguised as an old woman, he asked Frigga if there was anything in the world that had not taken the oath.

"All things agreed," she said, "except one little shrub that grows on the eastern side of Valhalla, home of the gods. It is called mistletoe. I thought it too young and feeble to ask it to take an oath."

When Loki heard this, he went off, resumed his natural shape, and brought a dart of mistletoe to the assembled gods. Present among them was the blind god Hoder, unable to join in the sport with Balder. "Why don't you throw something?" asked Loki.

"Because I am blind," answered Hoder, "and cannot see where he is standing."

"Come then, " said Loki. "Do like the rest of us. Throw this twig at Balder. I will direct your aim."

Hoder took the mistletoe, and under Loki's guidance he threw it at Balder. It pierced Balder and he fell down lifeless. For a long time the gods stood speechless. Then they lifted up their voices, weeping bitterly, and took Balder's body to the seashore, where his ship Ringhorn waited, and tried to launch it for his funeral pyre. But it would not move. So they sent for Hurrokin, a giantess, who gave it a push that made the whole earth shake. Then Balder's body was placed on the pyre aboard the boat. When his wife, Nanna, saw this, her heart burst and she too died. She was laid on the pyre, along with Balder's horse, and all were consumed by the flames.

For his crime Loki was banished from Asgard forever. To help the gods forget Loki's treachery and the loss of Balder, Aegir, god of the sea, invited them all to a feast in his coral caves at the bottom of the sea. The gods gladly accepted the invitation. Donning their richest garb, they arrived at the coral cave at the appointed time. Midway through the feast, Loki appeared cursing all the gods and finally slaying Funfent, Aegir's servant who had waited on the guests.

The gods again condemned Loki to banishment. Loki, however, continued to taunt the gods with their weaknesses and physical imperfections. Then Thor, in anger, lifted his magic hammer, and Loki fled the hall in fear.

Knowing he had lost all hope of ever returning to Asgard, Loki withdrew to the mountains. He built a hut with four doors, which he always left wide open to permit his hasty escape should the gods pursue him. Carefully laying his plans, he decided that if the gods ever came in search of him, he would rush down to the neighboring cataract and change himself into a salmon to avoid detection. As a salmon, Loki realized that although he could easily avoid any hook, it would be difficult for him to escape from a net. Haunted by this thought, he wondered if such an implement could be made. He began to work on one from twine when he saw the gods Thor and Odin in the distance. Knowing they had discovered his retreat and were about to make him prisoner, Loki threw his half-finished net into the fire and rushed out. He jumped into the waterfall, where in the shape of a salmon he hid among the stones.

The gods, finding the hut empty, were about to leave when they saw the remains of the burned net. They took it and began to drag the stream. Loki eluded them the first time by hiding at the bottom of the river between two stones. When the gods weighted the net and tried a second time, Loki escaped by jumping upstream. On a third attempt, however, they succeeded. Loki tried to escape, but Thor caught him in his hands. (The salmon, whose slipperiness is proverbial in northern countries, is noted for its slim tail, which the people attribute to Thor's tight grip on his foe Loki.)

Having captured Loki, the gods forced him to assume his natural shape, and dragged him into a cavern, where they bound him by the entrails of his son Narve. One of the fetters was passed under Loki's shoulders, and one under his loins. When he was securely bound hand and foot, the gods changed the entrails into iron. Then the giantess Skadi fastened a venomous serpent directly over Loki's head so that the poison would fall, drop by drop, upon his upturned face.

But Sigyn, Loki's faithful wife (it seems wives are expected to be faithful even to Evil gods as well as to Evil men), hurried with a cup to his side and gathered up the drops as they fell. She never left this position except when the cup was full. During her short absences to empty the cup, the drops of venom hitting Loki's face caused him such intense pain that he writhed in anguish, shaking the earth in his efforts to get free.

Loki will remain in this position until the twilight of the gods, or Ragnarok. Then Loki, the Fenris wolf, the Midgard serpent, and Hel, all his Evil children, will be set loose with their army of frost giants and other Evil beings. Heimdall, the watchman of the gods, will blow his horn, and the gods will prepare for the last battle. When the battle is over, with both gods and giants destroyed, "there will arise out of the sea another earth more lovely and verdant, with pleasant fields where the grain shall grow unsown."

While Loki has a distinct personality in Nordic mythology, his counterpart in Finnish mythology, Hiisi (or Lempo), is a rather indistinct being. He appears in the Finnish epic poem *The Kalevala*, where his name is also used as a general term for demons who haunt *Hittola* ("Demon's Domain"), a dreary region with charred and burned heaths and hills, not far from Pohjola, the Northland. Hiisi creates the Hiisi Elk, a magical animal which the hero Lemminkainen must subdue in order to win the Maiden of Pohjola as a wife. The Hiisi Elk has

> . . . a head of rotten timber,
> Horns composed of willow branches,

Feet of ropes the swamps which border,
Shins of stick from out the marches;
And his back was formed of fench stakes,
Sinews formed of dryest grass stalks,
Eyes of water lily flowers,
Ears of leaves of water lily,
And his hide was formed of pine bark,
And his flesh of rotten timber.

(W. F. Kirby translation)

Lemminkainen starts off in the best of spirits but is disappointed when he breaks his snowshoes and spear in pursuit of the Hiisi Elk. He finally subdues the beast by charms and magic prayers. When he is victorious, another task is assigned to him. He must bridle Hiisi's fire-breathing gelding, which he accomplishes. A third task is then assigned: He must kill the swan floating on the River of Death. Lemminkainen, however, is murdered before he can succeed, though later he is restored to life by his mother.

Actually the true demonic character in *The Kalevala* is not Hiisi but the gap-toothed Louhi, mistress of Pohjola and mother of the maiden whom Lemminkainen wishes to marry. Louhi has two daughters, the more lovely being the Maiden of Pohjola, who is wooed by all three heroes in the epic: Vainamoinen, Ilmarinen, and Lemminkainen. Finally, after Ilmarinen forges the magic Sampo for Louhi, he is given the bride. The Sampo makes Pohjola prosperous, and Vainamoinen decides to steal it for his land. He succeeds but is pursued by Louhi and her men. A great battle ensues in which the Sampo is lost in the lake, with only a few pieces left floating on the waters.

Louhi, enraged because her land has become barren after the loss of the Sampo, sends a plague to Vainamoinen's land, but the hero heals his people by the use of magic. Not satisfied, the Evil mistress then sends a great bear to ravish the herds, but Vainamoinen once again is victorious. Finally out of desperation Louhi steals the sun and moon as well as fire from all the hearths in Vainamoinen's land, but new fire is kindled by a thunderbolt from Ukko, the supreme god. Chains are then forged for Louhi by Ilmarinen, and out of fear, Louhi releases the sun and moon.

Chapter 10

Slavic Mythologies and Folklores

Byelobog and Chernobog represent the dual nature of
Good and Evil, while a host of demonic beings, such
as Likho, Thamar, and Vlad the Impaler, also known
as Dracula, haunt Slavic folklores.

In ancient Slavic mythology the gods Byelobog and Chernobog represented the dual nature of Good and Evil in the world. Byelobog went about in daytime helping travelers who had lost their way in the dark forest. He also bestowed wealth and fertility, helping the farmer have a good harvest. In White Russian popular legends, he is called Belun and is portrayed as an old man dressed in white and with a white beard. This later iconography obviously stems from Christian icons which portray God the Father as a white-bearded old man. Byelobog's evil counterpart, Chernobog, represents all Evil and darkness. In Western Slavic folklore, which also had contact with Christianity, Chernobog acquired many of the traits of the Christian Devil. Russian folklore, however, presents the best example in Likho ("Evil"), the one-eyed Evil spirit. In the Russian folktale *The One-Eyed Evil*, Likho is described as a tall woman, scrawny, crooked, and one-eyed. According to the folktale a blacksmith and a tailor went in search of Likho to see what she was really like. A short time after they arrived at Likho's house, she killed the tailor and served him to the blacksmith for dinner. The blacksmith, in order to save himself, told Likho that he could restore her lost eye if only she would let him tie her with some ropes. Likho agreed and was easily tied up but just as easily broke her bonds. A stronger rope was brought. She was again tied and this time held fast as the blacksmith took out her other eye, making her completely blind. He escaped by donning a sheepskin (as Odysseus did in Homer's *Odyssey* when he escaped from the one-eyed Cyclops). The blacksmith was nearly caught while fleeing when his hand stuck to a golden ax in a tree. To free himself he had to cut off his hand since Likho, although blinded, was close behind him. When he arrived at his village, he told everyone what had happened: He had seen

Likho, who not only left him with just one hand, but also "ate up his companion."

This Russian folktale introduces us to one of a host of female demons which haunt Slavic folklore. In fact Slavic folklore often identifies the demonic element with females, though of course male demons also figure among the large number of evildoers. Among the most famous of the female variety is Baba Yaga, a cannibalistic ogress who kidnaps children and eats them. Baba Yaga usually lives in a hut which stands on hens' legs. Sometimes it faces the forest, sometimes the path, and sometimes it moves from place to place. In some Russian folktales Baba Yaga's hut has a railing around it made of sticks surmounted by human skulls, which glow at night from candles placed inside.

From her description Baba Yaga would not arouse any physical passion in the male, though many of her female-demon counterparts in Slavic folklore do. Thamar, who is an Evil queen in the legend of Russian Georgia, feasted with her many lovers, whom she threw into the river from a parapet of her castle.

Queen Thamar's castle was located near the mighty Terek River. From her window at night came the sound of her "enchanting voice, whose song lured traveler, merchant, warrior or peasant to see her within the castle." When the gates to the castle were opened and the wanderer entered, he found himself in a luxurious room where Thamar, "richly bedecked in brocade and jewels, reclined voluptuously on a couch." She feasted with the man, locking him in "passionate embraces," but the next morning "the waters of the Terek River would bear away his corpse." From her window could be heard the whispered cry, "Farewell."

Another "romantic" counterpart of Thamar is the Rusalka, a female water-spirit of a drowned girl. Two types of Rusalka are met with in various Slavic folktales: the northern one, a demonic being somewhat pale, who entices men with her songs and then drowns them as Thamar did; and the southern version, an attractive girl who also entices men, but she truly loves them. When a man dies in her arms, it is considered a blessing.

The Rusalkai (plural of Rusalka) live part of the year in water, but when the sun is too hot in summertime, they seek green trees near the river as their homes. In Slavic folklore green trees are believed to be the abode of the dead from whose souls the Rusalkai derived.

The male counterpart of the Rusalka is the Vodyanik. The Vodyanik can assume many forms and shapes. Often he appears as a bald old man with a fat belly, wearing a cap of reeds and a belt of rushes. When he appears in a village, he assumes a human shape, but one can tell he is a Vodyanik because water oozes from the left side of his coat. When not in some other form, he lives in the deeper parts of the water, preferably near mills with stone-built courtyards where he keeps animals. In the daytime he usually stays in the water, but at night he comes up and can be seen combing his green hair.

Closely associated with the Rusalka is the Vila, another female spirit in Slavic folklore, often the ghost of a girl who died before her wedding day, or was a suicide, or died unbaptized.

A Vila appears at night, enticing men to their doom by inviting them to the graveyard. This motif was used in the ballet *Giselle, ou Les Wilis* (1841), by the French composer Adolphe Charles Adam (1803–56), who based his scenario on a story by Théophile Gautier and Vernoy Saint-Georges. They in turn had adapted it from Heinrich Heine's *De l'Allemagne*.

In the ballet, Giselle kills herself when she discovers that her intended husband Loys is in reality a prince named

Albrecht, who is betrothed to another woman. Giselle returns from the dead as a Vila and is ordered by Myrtha, Queen of the Vilas, to entice Albrecht to his death. Giselle instead leads him to a cross, knowing it will protect him from all harm. Myrtha, furious that her command has not been obeyed, orders all the other Vilas to ensnare Albrecht, but Giselle begs Myrtha to spare him. The queen refuses and Albrecht nearly collapses from exhaustion after being drawn into a death-dance. He is saved when the sound of distant morning church bells scatters the spirits. Albrecht then looks to Giselle, whose grave opens to receive her, leaving him alone.

The legend of the Vila was taken up again in the first opera of Giacomo Puccini, *Le Villi* (1884), with a libretto by Ferdinando Fontana. Puccini's opera was composed as an entry in a contest, but it failed to win. Arrigo Boito, a composer and librettist, was impressed by the work, and raised funds for its first production.

The opera takes place in the Black Forest of Germany. The betrothal of Robert and Anna is being celebrated. Shortly after, Robert goes to seek his fortune, soon forgetting his wife, who dies of a broken heart. When Robert later returns, expecting to find Anna waiting, he is instead confronted by her apparition. She denounces him for his cruelty. A horde of Vilas appear, dancing around Robert, until he falls dead at their feet.

Though the Vila has received much attention in European music, the Dziwozony, or wild woman, in Polish folklore never seems to have reached that stage. A Dziwozony has a cold heart but is extremely physically passionate at the same time. She is tall with a thin face and long, disheveled hair, flinging her breasts over her shoulders in order to run. If she comes upon an adult in the forest, she usually tickles the person to death. Younger people are often made into her lovers.

The forest, which is the haunt of the Dziwozony, is also the haunt of the Leshy, a forest-spirit, often of a mischievous nature, who can assume any shape. When a Leshy is in the mood, he removes stones and signposts, making the traveler lose his way, though the Leshy will then lead the person back onto the right path after having played his prank. If one were caught by a Leshy, a certain rite was ordained which would make the Leshy's spells useless: The person had to sit down under a tree trunk, remove all clothes, and put them on backward, remembering to put the left shoe on the right foot.

Slavic folktales say the Leshy is the offspring of a demon and a woman. Sometimes the Leshy seduces a girl, taking her in the forest where she is raped. Occasionally the Leshy substitutes an ugly spirit child for a real one. At the beginning of October the Leshys traditionally disappear, indicating they have died or gone into some type of hibernation until the following spring, when they reappear.

Much more troublesome than the Leshy is the Vlkodlak, or wolf-man, who is either born as a wolf-man or subsequently transformed into one by witchcraft. It is believed that a child born feet first and with teeth will become a Vlkodlak. If the person is later transformed into a wolf-man, only the person who cast the spell can undo it. A Vlkodlak can also appear in the form of another animal, such as a hen, horse, cow, dog, or cat. It attacks cattle, sucking cows, mares, and sheep, and strangles horses. The only remedy against the Vlkodlak is the Kresnik, a Good spirit who battles demonic forces.

In popular imagination the nearest association to the wolf-man is the vampire, particularly Dracula, the generally known name of Vlad the Impaler (*c.* 1431–76), a historical Romanian tyrant who is known in popular writings for his vampirism. Various theories have been advanced about the truth of Vlad the Vampire, or Vlad Tepes. According to an official Romanian Communist Government Tourist Agency, "the real Dracula fought for the cause of the Romanian people." Yet older legend has credited this "hero" of the people with the most bizarre, horrendous deeds. In German, Russian, Hungarian, and Italian folklore, the deeds of Dracula are copiously recorded, though no mention is made of his vampirism.

A few of the legends surrounding the sadistic tyrant tell how he punished those who in any way offended him. For example, when a group of Turkish envoys did not remove their turbans in his presence, he had their turbans nailed to their heads. Dracula often dined outdoors amid the screams of his impaled victims hung upon stakes around the dinner table. Once a guest complained of the stench of the decaying bodies. Dracula had the guest impaled on a stake much higher than the others in order to die out of the range of their odors. Another tale tells how Dracula invited some beggars into his castle, fed them, and told them he could end all their troubles if they wished. They agreed, and he had them shut indoors and burned alive.

However, Dracula in modern folklore is noted for his vampirism, stemming from Bram Stoker's novel *Dracula* (1897). Stoker's novel in turn has been used as the basis of numerous films, beginning with a silent film, *Nosferatu* (1923), and continuing through many versions, including the classic *Dracula* (1931) starring Bela Lugosi, who became identified with the role in movies. *The Fearless Vampire Killers* (1967), by the Polish director Roman Polanski, gives Dracula the name Count Von Krolock, but he still has all the trappings of the old vampire count.

Chapter 11

Siberian Mythology and Folklore

Erlik, Schulman, and Satan are some of the names
the Devil assumes, but his purpose is always the same,
the destruction of mankind.

Once Ulgen, a creator-god in Siberian mythology, came down from heaven upon the waters. He desired to create the earth, though he did not know how to accomplish the feat. Suddenly Erlik, a man, appeared and told him how it could be done. With Ulgen's approval Erlik dived down into the water's depths and brought up a piece of earth, part of which he gave to Ulgen and part of which he kept himself. Ulgen created the earth with his part, while Erlik's piece formed the swamps and bogs of the earth.

A variant of the myth tells how Ulgen saw some mud with humanlike features floating on the ocean. He gave it life and the name Erlik. At first Erlik was Ulgen's friend and brother, but later he became his enemy and the Devil.

In a myth told by the Black Tartars, the Kudai (seven spirits who watch over men's destinies) supplied souls to the lifeless forms created by the god Pajana, who had made them from the earth. Seeing that they lacked life, Pajana had gone to the Kudai to get life-giving spirits to instill into his new creations. He left a naked dog to guard them while he was away. Erlik came and said he would cover the dog with golden hair if the animal would give him the soulless bodies. The dog agreed. Erlik then spit on the bodies. When Pajana saw what happened he turned the bodies inside out. That is why man's inside is filled with filth.

While the myths told by different Siberian tribes vary, there is general agreement that Erlik will be destroyed at the end of the world. In the meantime, however, Erlik-Khan ("Great Khan") is Lord of the Dead who sends out his fellow Evil spirits to seize the souls of those who have sinned, bringing them to judgment.

One Buriat myth tells how the hero Mu-monto visited the land ruled by Erlik-Khan, demanding back a horse he had sacrificed at his father's death. To reach the land of the dead, Mu-monto went due north and found a rock, which he lifted. "Come here," it said.

A black fox suddenly appeared from under the stone and led him the rest of the way. When he arrived, Mu-Monto saw all sorts of punishments meted out to those who had been Evil in life. Thieves were bound, liars had their lips sewed together, adulterous wives were tied to thornbushes, and those who had been false in their professions were put in boiling pitch. He also saw that a poor woman, who was Good in her life, was now living a life of luxury while an Evil rich woman now lived in rags.

In a Tartar variant the black fox of the Buriat myth is identified as the daughter of Erlik-Khan. A hero, Komdei-Mirgan, went to hunt the black fox. He did not achieve his objective but instead had his leg broken. While he tried to get up, Yelbegen, a monster with nine heads and riding a forty-horned ox, cut off Komdei-Mirgan's head and brought it to the Land of the Dead. Komdei-Mirgan's sister Kubaiko traveled to the underworld to retrieve the head of her brother. After numerous adventures she succeeded, and with the Water of Life obtained from God, she brought her brother back to life.

The Land of the Dead in Siberian mythology shows the conglomerate nature of its beliefs, since it reveals Christian, Islamic, and Buddhist concepts in its description of the punishments and rewards meted out to the dead. As in these other mythologies, the Devil is known by various names.

Schulman, another name for the Devil, once created three suns in order to burn the earth, which had been newly created by Burkhan-Bakshai, another creator-god in Siberian mythology. God countered by covering the unpeopled earth with water. Only one sun remained in the sky while the other two were plunged down to the bottomless pit where Schulman was also sent as punishment.

Erlik or Schulman, the Devil, is constantly appearing in Siberian myths, along with various creator-gods, forming an important part of the cosmic order. In the mythology of the Yakuts, which is also part of Siberian mythology, native beliefs regarding creation and the Devil are wedded to Christian concepts.

According to one myth, Yryn-Ajy-Tojon, a creator-god, saw a bladder floating on the waters and asked what it was. The bladder replied that it was Satan, who lived on the earth under the water.

"If there is really earth under the water, then bring me a piece of it," replied Yryn-Ajy-Tojon.

Satan dived under the water and returned with a piece of earth. It was blessed by Yryn-Ajy-Tojon and placed upon the waters, where he sat on it. Satan, angry, tried to drown the god by stretching the earth, but the more he pulled, the larger the earth became until it covered the waters.

The name *Satan* of course reveals part of the Christian overlay to this primitive myth. This does not obscure the fact that the act of creation and the introduction of Evil in the world is viewed as an integral part of the order of the world. Without Evil there would be no earth.

An even stronger resemblance to Christian beliefs is found in the Siberian myth of Torongoi and Edji, the first people, who are equivalent to Adam and Eve in Biblical myth.

Torongoi and Edji were created with fur on their bodies to keep them warm. They were told they could eat fruit from the branches that pointed toward the sunrise but were forbidden to eat from the branches that pointed to the sunset. To help the couple, God sent a dog to bite the Devil if he came, and a snake to attack him. When God returned to heaven, the Devil crept into the skin of the sleeping snake and tempted the first woman. She, as in the Biblical myth, also made her husband eat, and both then became frightened as they saw their fur fall from their bodies.

When God came down from heaven, Torongoi said Edji had made him eat the fruit; Edji said the snake made her eat the fruit; the snake said the Devil was inside him; and the dog said he hadn't seen anything.

The end of the Devil known variously as Erlik, Schulman, and Satan is given in a Tartar myth. Ulgen, the creator-god, will send Maidere (a hero derived from the Buddhist Maitreya, the loving or coming Buddha) to teach the love of God and convert mankind. Out of envy Erlik will kill Maidere, but the hero's blood will cover the whole earth and burst into flames which will rise to the heavens. Ulgen will call the dead to arise, and Erlik and his cohorts will be destroyed.

Chapter 12

Hindu Mythology and Folklore

Brahma, Vishnu, and Siva act out the cosmic becoming and the destruction of the universe, while Mahadevi, the great goddess, combines both demonic and beneficent aspects in her various roles.

Brahma created by his thought. When he concentrated, darkness became manifest, and demons were born from his thigh. He then left that body, which became night. Still desiring to create, Brahma took another body filled with goodness. From his mouth were born the gods. He then abandoned that body, and it became day. Day is Good, belonging to the gods, but night is Evil, belonging to the demons. Brahma also created twilight and dawn.

This brief summary of one of the creation myths in Hinduism, found in the *Vishnu Purana*, credits creation to Brahma, who makes pairs of opposites, Good and Evil, light and dark. However Brahma is not all powerful, since he must act out of his own *karma* (the cumulative force of his actions, Good or Bad, which predetermines the course of his present existence).

Brahma in present-day Hinduism is often called the first of the gods, the framer of the universe, and the guardian of the world. In the ancient *Vedas*, however, he is not named directly; the creator is called Hiranya-garbha or Prajapati ("lord of creatures"). The title was later applied to Brahma as well as to his sons, who in Hindu mythology are progenitors of the human race.

The various accounts of the origin of Brahma differ considerably. In the Hindu epic poem *The Mahabharata*, Brahma is said to have issued from the lotus that sprang from the navel of the god Vishnu. In another text Brahma is said to have lived in a cosmic egg for a thousand years and then burst out. Seeing that the earth was sunk beneath the waters, Brahma assumed the form of a boar (in later Hindu writings this role is assigned to Vishnu as one of his avatars, or incarnations). He dived to the bottom of the waters and raised the earth upon his tusks. After this Brahma continued the work of creation.

Concerning Brahma's role as supreme creator of the universe, Ralph Waldo Emerson, the American poet, wrote in *Brahma* (1857):

> If the red slayer think he slays,
>   Or if the slain think he is slain,
> They know not well the subtle ways
>   I keep, and pass, and turn again.
>
> Far or forgot to me is near;
>   Shadow and sunlight are the same;
> The vanished gods to me appear;
>   And one to me are shame and fame.
>
> They reckon ill who leave me out;
>   When me they fly, I am the wings;
> I am the doubter and the doubt,
>   And I the hymn the Brahmin sings.
>
> The strong gods pine for my abode,
>   And pine in vain the sacred Seven;
> But thou, meek lover of the good!
>   Find me, and turn thy back on heaven.

When Emerson was questioned on the meaning of his poem, since many readers were upset by the imagery and use of an alien god, he said to his daughter, "Tell them to say Jehovah instead of Brahma."

Numerous myths are told of Brahma in various Hindu texts. Once Brahma, as Apava ("who sports in the waters"), formed two beings from his body, a male, Viraj, and a female, Satarupa ("the hundred-formed"). After her creation Brahma desired her.

"How beautiful you are," he said to his daughter.

Satarupa turned to avoid Brahma's lustful look, but the god sprouted a second head. As she passed to the left, two other heads appeared. At last Satarupa sprang up to the sky, and Brahma grew a fifth head to view her. Satarupa then came down and the two made love, producing off-

spring which later populated the earth. She became
Brahma's wife.

Brahma did not keep his fifth head, for it was cut off by
the god Siva. When the holy sages were assembled at
Brahma-pura, the heavenly city of Brahma on Mount
Meru, they asked Brahma to diplay his true nature.
Brahma, influenced by a delusion brought upon him by a
demon, and obscured by spiritual darkness (gods and people in Hindu mythology share the same virtues and
faults), said, "I am the womb of the universe, without the
beginning or end, and the sole and self-existent lord; and
he who does not worship me shall never attain beatitude."

On hearing this reply, Kratus (a form of the god
Vishnu) smiled and said, "Had thou not been misled by ignorance, thou wouldst not have made an assertion con-
trary to truth; for I am the framer of the universe, the
source of life, the unborn, eternal and supreme. Had I not
willed it, creation would not have taken place."

The two gods then fought, finally agreeing to let the
sacred writings, the *Vedas*, decide the issue. The *Vedas*
declared that Siva was the creator, preserver, and destroyer. Siva then appeared and Brahma's fifth head asked
Siva to worship him. Siva assumed a horrible form and
cut off Brahma's fifth head with the thumb of his left
hand.

Vishnu and Siva are among the most popular gods
in present-day Hinduism. In the ancient *Rig-Veda*, however, Vishnu is not of first rank, but in later works such as
The Mahabharata and the *Puranas* he is often the second
member of a triad, the embodiment of Satwa-guna, the
quality of mercy and goodness which displays itself as the
preserving power, the self-existent, all-pervading spirit.
The worshipers of Vishnu recognize him as the supreme
being from whom all things originate.

Vishnu's preserving and restoring power has been manifest in the world in various avatars ("descents"), commonly called incarnations, in which a portion of his divine nature was embodied in a human or animal form. Each avatar is sent to correct some Evil in the world. Ten are traditionally accepted, though some texts say twenty-two, while others say they are numberless. The most popular are Rama, the seventh, and Krishna, the eighth, both of which are worshiped as gods.

In his first avatar, Matsya ("a fish"), Vishnu took the form of a fish and saved Manu, one of the progenitors of the human race, from the great Flood which destroyed the world. Manu found a small fish which asked him for protection. The fish grew rapidly and Manu recognized it as Vishnu incarnate. When the great Flood came, Vishnu as Matsya led the ark over the waters and saved Manu and the seeds of all living things. (There are various accounts of this myth, with Vishnu appearing only in the later ones.)

As the second avatar, Kurma ("the tortoise"), Vishnu took the form of Kurma to recover valuable objects lost in the great Flood. During the Churning of the Ocean, when the gods and demons fought for Amrita, immortality, Vishnu also appeared as Kurma and aided the gods.

In his third avatar, Vishnu became Varaha ("the boar") to rid the world of the demon-giant Hiranyaksha ("golden eye"), who had dragged the earth to the depths of the ocean. Vishnu fought the demon for a thousand years before he slew him. In the epic poem *The Ramayana*, it says that the god "Brahma became a boar and raised up the earth." The feat was later ascribed to Vishnu by his worshipers.

As Nara-sinha ("man-lion"), the fourth avatar, Vishnu became Nara-sinha to rid the world of the demon Hiranya-kasipu ("golden dress"), who had control over the three worlds—heaven, atmosphere and earth—for a

million years. The demon obtained control from either
Brahma or Siva (accounts vary). The demon's son Prah-
lada worshiped Vishnu, which naturally upset his father.
Hiranya-kasipu then tried to kill his son, but the boy was
protected by Vishnu. In a scornful tone Hiranya-kasipu
asked his son if Vishnu was in a pillar supporting the hall
of his palace. The boy said, "Yes." The demon announced, "I will kill him!" and he struck the pillar. But
Vishnu stepped out of the pillar as Nara-sinha and tore
Hiranya-kasipu to shreds.

Vamana ("the dwarf") was Vishnu's fifth avatar. King
Bali ("offering"), through his devotions and severe austerities, acquired control over the three worlds (heaven, atmosphere, and earth). He so humbled all the gods that they
asked Vishnu to protect them from Bali's power. In the
form of Vamana, Vishnu came to earth and asked Bali to
be allowed to make three steps ("the three strides of
Vishnu" mentioned in the *Rig-Veda*). As much land as
Vamana could cover would then belong to him. Since
Vamana was a dwarf, Bali consented. Then Vishnu took
two gigantic steps, striding over heaven and earth, but out
of respect for Bali, he stopped short of the underworld—
leaving that domain for the king. There are numerous
variants in Hindu texts of the story of the three steps
taken by the god. Bali is sometimes called Maha-bali
("great Bali").

Parasu-rama ("Rama with the ax") was the sixth avatar.
Parasu-rama came to earth to deliver the Brahmins
(priests) from the control of the Kshatriyas (the warrior
caste). He is said to have cleared the earth of the Kshatriyas twenty-one times. In his early life Parasu-rama was
under the protection of the god Siva, who taught him the
use of arms and gave him the *parasu* ("ax"), whence came
his name. The first act told of him in the Hindu epic poem
The Mahabharata relates to his mortal father, Jamadagni

("fire-eating"). Jamadagni was a king who ordered his sons to kill their mother, Runuka, because she was "defiled by unworthy thoughts." Four of Jamadagni's sons would not kill their mother, and as a result the king cursed them, turning them into idiots. The fifth son, Parasu-rama, struck off his mother's head with an ax. Jamadagni then asked Parasu-rama what gift or request he wished. Parasu-rama begged his father to restore his mother to life and his brothers to sanity. The request was granted.

Rama ("charming"), the seventh avatar, is regarded as a full incarnation of Vishnu, while the others were only partial ones. Rama's tale is told in numerous Hindu works, the most famous being the epic poem *The Ramayana*, which is found in numerous retellings throughout India. In his role as a god, Rama, along with his wife, Sita, is worshiped in certain parts of India.

In the eighth avatar, Krishna ("the dark one"), the god came to save the world from "Evil spirits" who committed "great crimes." Among the most famous was the demon-king Kamsa.

Buddha ("enlightened") was the ninth avatar. With the rise of Buddhism as a reaction against Hinduism, the Hindus incorporated Buddha as one of the incarnations of Vishnu. Buddha came to draw people away from Vedic sacrifice so that the world would decay at its appointed time.

Kalki ("impure," or "sinful"), the tenth avatar, has not yet occurred. Vishnu is to appear at the end of the world, seated on a white horse, with drawn sword blazing like a comet, for the final destruction of the wicked, the renovation of creation, and the restoration of purity.

All the deities mentioned—Brahma, Siva, and Vishnu—are male, but India also possesses Mahadevi ("the great goddess"), who is one of the most ancient deities still worshiped in Hinduism. Traces of her worship date back to prehistoric times. She was taken into the Hindu pantheon and wedded to the god Siva, being made his *shakti*, or female energy.

Mahadevi assumes many roles; among them is Sati ("the good woman"). Daughter of Daksha, she is married to the god Siva. To prove her love for Siva she burned herself alive at Jwala-mukhi ("mouth of fire"), a volcano in the lower Himalayas, north of Punjab. Today the place is a site of pilgrimage. When Siva embraced the body of his wife, it took the god Vishnu to cut her out of Siva's hold. Fifty pieces of her bodily remains including the *yoni* ("womb"), the female organ, and Siva's *linga* ("phallus") were then scattered, each becoming a place of worship.

As Parvati ("the mountaineer"), Devi is the constant companion and loving wife of Siva, often engaging in love-making. On one occasion Siva reproached Parvati for the darkness of her skin. She was so upset by the remark that she went to live alone in the forest where she performed austerities. The god Brahma, in reward for her austerities, said he would grant her any wish. Parvati asked that her complexion be golden. She was then called Gauri ("cow-colored," or "brilliant") and became known as the goddess of crops and as the harvest bride; or Uma ("light"), the golden goddess, personification of light and beauty. As Sandhya she is viewed as twilight personified. (In some texts Sandhya is believed to be the daughter of the god Brahma.)

Jaganamata ("the mother of the world") is the personification of the goddess as the great mother, recalling her early worship as Mahadevi, while as the goddess Durga ("the inaccessible"), she fought the great buffalo-demon Mahisha. The demon, having performed penance in favor of Brahma or Siva, obtained great power and took over control of the three worlds, dethroning Indra, the atmospheric god, as well as sending the other gods fleeing to Brahma for help.

At a meeting of the gods, "their united energies" produced a woman, Durga, "more dangerous than all the gods and demons." (In a variant account Durga already existed as the wife of Siva and came to the aid of the gods.) Durga set out to destroy the buffalo-demon. At first she sent Kalaratri ("dark night"), a female whose beauty bewitched the three worlds. Mahisha, even though moved by her charms, came after Kalaratri, who of course was a form of Durga, and "she took the unassailable form of fire." When the demon in the form of a buffalo saw her standing before him, blazing with her great magic power of illusion, he made himself as large as Mount Meru. The demon then sent an army, but it was reduced to ashes by the fire. Mahisha next sent 30,000 giants, which made Kalaratri rush to Durga (we must accept the fact that these figures can be in two places at the same time as well as in two forms that are part of one being). As Durga sat on Mount Vindhya, the demon's troops hurled arrows as thick as the drops of rain in a storm. In return Durga threw a weapon which carried away the arms of many of the giants. Mahisha then hurled a flaming dart at the goddess, which she turned aside. He sent another and she stopped it by a hundred arrows. His next arrow was aimed at Durga's heart, but this one too was stopped. At last the two came together and Durga seized Mahisha, setting her foot on his chest, but Mahisha disengaged himself and renewed the battle.

This battle continued for some time until Durga pierced Mahisha with her trident. He reeled to and fro, and again assumed his original form, that of a giant with a thousand arms, having a weapon in each. Durga seized him by his arms, carried him into the air, then threw him to the ground. Seeing that the fall did not kill him, she pierced his chest with an arrow. Blood began to flow from his mouth and he died.

In Indian art Durga is often portrayed as a golden-colored woman with ten arms, being called Dashbhuja ("ten-armed") because of her destruction of Mahisha. In one hand she often holds a spear which is piercing Mahisha. With another hand she holds the tail of a serpent, with another the hair of Mahisha, whose chest the snake is biting. Her other hands are filled with weapons and she rides a lion.

Another important manifestation of the goddess Devi is Kali ("the black one"). Kali was sent to earth to destroy a host of demons, but in her rampage of death and destruction she also killed men and women. The gods, horrified that if she were not stopped, all life would cease, pleaded with her to stop, but to no avail. Finally her husband Siva threw himself down amid the bodies of the dead. When Kali realized she was trampling upon her husband, she regained her senses. As a sign of shame she stuck out her tongue, and Kali is often thus portrayed in Indian art.

Other attributes of Kali are fanged teeth, matted hair, and four red eyes. In two arms she holds the symbols of death, a noose to strangle her victims and a hook to drag them. In her other hands she holds the symbols of life, a prayerbook and prayerbeads. Kali also wears a skull necklace, corpse earrings, and is surrounded by serpents, which according to some interpretations shows her mastery over the male.

The city of Calcutta received its name from Kalighat ("the riverbank of Kali"), where her worshipers descend into the sacred Ganges River. In earlier times human sacrifices were made to the goddess. Members of the cult, called "thugs" (from which came our English word), robbed and strangled their victims before sacrificing them to the goddess. The cult was suppressed in the last century.

Kali is assisted in her work by the demoness Dakini, who feeds upon human flesh.

Chapter 13

Buddhist Mythology and Folklore

Mara, the Evil One, tempts the Buddha, only to be defeated by him, since Good and Evil proceed from the person.

Once, a long time ago, the Future Buddha appeared on earth as a woodpecker. He was not an ordinary woodpecker, but one of the most beautiful birds in the whole forest. It happened one day, as he was rambling through the forest, that he came upon a lion, who lay on the ground in great pain.

"What is the matter?" said the woodpecker to the King of the Forest. "Are you ill?"

"Ah, yes," replied the lion. "I have a bone stuck in my throat, like the point of an arrow. It causes me great pain. I can neither swallow it nor throw it up. Can you help me?"

"Yes," replied the woodpecker, who then took a large piece of wood lying on the ground. "Open your mouth," instructed the woodpecker, "as wide as you can."

The lion opened his mouth, and the woodpecker placed the large beam between the two rows of grinning teeth. He then entered the lion's mouth. With his small beak he took up the bone fragment, drawing it out. As he left the mouth of the lion, he removed the wood beam.

The lion thanked the bird, who went on his way. Some time later it happened that the woodpecker was flying about, looking for some food. He saw the lion he had helped feasting on the flesh of a young antelope which the lion had just slaughtered. Blood covered the lion's paws, and his teeth were dripping with it. The lion greedily ate the antelope, not noticing the woodpecker. So the bird approached the lion and, like a beggar, asked for some food.

"Do you come here to insult me!" the lion replied angrily to the woodpecker. "Wasn't it enough that I didn't eat you when you were in my mouth?"

The woodpecker took flight at these words, and the lion continued to eat his victim. A forest-spirit saw what happened and went to the woodpecker.

"Why didn't you punish the lion for his injury to you?" the forest-spirit said, knowing the woodpecker was a Future Buddha and had power over all the animals in the forest.

"It is out of mercy, not with the desire of gain, that the virtuous take care of a person in distress," replied the woodpecker, "nor do they mind whether the other person understands this or not."

The above is a retelling of "The Fable of the Woodpecker," one of the *Jatakas*, or *(Birth-) Stories of Former Lives of the Buddha*. The fable illustrates the Buddhist doctrine that good actions are performed regardless of whether they are appreciated by the recipient. It also illustrates that "a virtuous person is incapable of betaking himself to evil, even though provoked, having never learnt to do so."

In Buddhism, then, Evil and Good proceed from the person. In *The Dhammapada*, a Buddhist work traditionally ascribed to the Buddha himself, it is neatly put:

> By self alone is evil done,
> By self is one disgraced;
> By self is evil left undone,
> By self alone is he purified;
> Purity and impurity belong to self;
> No man can purify another.

This Evil spoken of by the Buddha, the Enlightened One, is given its best personification in the image of Mara ("the killer"). Originally Mara was a Hindu demon, Namuche, who constantly fought against the sky-god, Indra. He was a mischievous spirit who prevented rain and produced drought, since his name means "not letting go the waters." In many Hindu myths Indra forces Namuche to send down his fertilizing rains and restore the earth. Mara is also called Papiyan ("more wicked," or "very wicked") and Varsavarti ("he who fulfills desires"). In this last version his true nature is revealed: the thirst for existence, the thirst for pleasure, and the thirst for power. It is therefore quite appropriate that when the Future Buddha was on his way to attain Buddhahood ("Enlightenment"), the archfiend Mara should be disturbed and appear as the Tempter of the Future Buddha.

Mara, who was Lord of the Five Earthly Desires, skilled in the arts of warfare, and foe to those who seek deliverance from the world, was sad. He had three very beautiful daughters who could inflame a man with love, destroying the man's desire to attain Buddhahood. The three came before their father.

"Tell us what makes you so sad," they asked Mara.

"The world now has a great spiritual leader who is wise and strong," Mara replied unhappily. "His object is to gain mastery over the world, to ruin and destroy my kingdom. I am myself unequal to him, for all men will believe in him and all find refuge in the way of his salvation. Then my land will be deserted and unoccupied. But if I can divert him from his purpose, I can save my kingdom."

Seizing his bow and five arrows, surrounded by his numerous male and female attendants, Mara went to the grove where the Future Buddha was seated in meditation under the Bo tree.

"Get up quickly," Mara said to the Future Buddha. "Your death is at hand. You may practice your own religious system, but give up this effort to deliver others! Save yourself only! If you do not arise, I will shoot this arrow of death at you."

In the face of these threats, the Future Buddha remained unmoved. He had no doubt; no fear was present. Then Mara let fly an arrow while his three daughters approached the Future Buddha to inflame him with sensual desire. The Future Buddha, however, did not regard the arrow, nor look at the three young women.

Seeing that his first attempt had failed, Mara, the Evil One, assembled his army. Each being took on a menacing form, some holding spears, others diamond swords, and some snatched up trees, roots and all. Some had heads like horses, others like fishes, others like asses, snakes, dragons, and beasts of every kind. They all arranged themselves before the Future Buddha, threatening every moment to destroy him, fiercely staring, grinning, flying tumultuously, bounding here and there. The Future Buddha, silently beholding them, watched as one would watch the games of children.

The army of Mara took up weapons, but the soldiers were powerless to use them; their flying spears, lances, and javelins stuck fast in space, refusing to descend. The angry thunderdrops and mighty hail were changed into five-colored lotus flowers, while the foul poisons of the dragons were turned into perfumes. Then all the Evil creatures were wounded by their own weapons.

At last Mara caused a darkness to descend, but the darkness disappeared before the Future Buddha, as night vanishes before the sun.

"Siddharta," Mara cried, "arise from thy seat. It does not belong to thee. It belongs to me."

"Mara," the Future Buddha replied, "you have not fulfilled the Ten Perfections. This seat belongs to me, for I have fulfilled the Ten Perfections."

Mara then called his demon army to witness his next pronouncement. The Future Buddha said, "I have no animate witnesses present." He stretched out his right hand toward the earth and said, "Will you bear me witness?"

The earth thundered back, "I bear you witness."

At this reply Mara's mighty elephant fell upon its knees to worship the Future Buddha, and the followers of Mara fled in all directions. Voices from heaven were heard saying, "Behold the great spiritual leader. His mind unmoved by hatred; the host of the wicked one has not overawed him. He is pure and wise, loving and full of mercy."

Having put Mara to flight, the Future Buddha gave himself up to meditation. All the miseries of the world, the Evils produced by Evil deeds, and the sufferings arising from them passed before his mental eye. He thought:

"Surely if living creatures saw the results of all their Evil deeds, they would turn away from them in disgust. But selfhood blinds them and they cling to their obnoxious desires. They crave for pleasures and they cause pain; when death destroys their individuality, they find no peace; their thirst for existence abides and their selfhood reappears in new births. Thus they continue to move in the coil and can find no escape from the hell of their own making. And how empty are their pleasures, how vain are their endeavors! Hollow like the plantain-tree and without contents like the bubble.

"The world is full of sin and sorrow, because it is full of error. Men go astray because they think that delusion is better than truth. Rather than truth they follow error, which is pleasant to look at in the beginning but then causes anxiety, tribulation, and misery."

Then the Buddha, the Enlightened One, saw the four noble truths which point the path that leads to Nirvana. The Buddha said:

"The first noble truth is the existence of sorrow. Birth is sorrowful, growth is sorrowful, illness is sorrowful, and death is sorrowful. Sad it is to be joined with that which we do not like. Sadder still is the separation from that which we love, and painful is the craving for that which cannot be obtained.

"The second noble truth is the cause of suffering. The cause of suffering is lust. The surrounding world affects sensation and begets a craving thirst, which clamors for immediate satisfaction. The illusion of self originates and manifests itself in a cleaving to things. The desire to live for the enjoyment of self entangles us in the net of sorrow. Pleasures are the bait, and the result is pain.

"The third noble truth is the cessation of sorrow. He who conquers self will be free from lust. He no longer craves, and the flames of desire find no material to feed upon. Thus they will be extinguished.

"The fourth noble truth is the eightfold path that leads to the cessation of sorrow. There is salvation for him whose self disappears before Truth, whose will is bent upon what he ought to do, whose sole desire is the performance of his duty. He who is wise will enter this path and make an end of sorrow. The eightfold path is: (1) right comprehension; (2) right resolutions; (3) right speech; (4) right acts; (5) right way of earning a livelihood; (6) right efforts; (7) right thoughts; and (8) right state of a peaceful mind."

The above Eight-Faced Path of Buddhism is the Dharma (the "truth"), for "the existence of self is an illusion, and there is no wrong in this world, no vice, no sin, except what flows from the assertion of self. The attainment of truth is possible only when self is recognized as an illusion. Righteousness can be practiced only when we have freed our mind from the passions of egotism. Perfect peace can dwell only where all vanity has disappeared."

Buddhism's basic philosophical nature (it does not, for example, have a belief in a personal creator-God) does not prevent it from having a rich mythological tradition: Gods, demons, heavens, and hells abound, filling its temples and sacred writings. In Buddhism's use of various gods and demons, their original natures are often changed to suit Buddhist beliefs. Thus the gods are inferior to the Buddhas, those who have achieved Enlightenment. Of the numerous deities adapted by Buddhism from other mythologies, those connected with India, the land where

Buddhism had its birth, supply a rich assortment. The atmospheric god Indra, for example, is found in both Hindu
and Buddhist belief, but the great god Siva and his wife
Parvati, usually called Mahakala and Mahakali, become
the inferior doorkeepers of the Buddha. Often the terrifying aspects of the Hindu gods is intensified in Buddhism.

Thus Ushas, who is the goddess of dawn in Hindu
belief, becomes a fierce goddess, Marishai, with a third
eye, three hideous faces, and ten threatening arms. Yama,
the Hindu god of the dead, is called Dharmaraja, although
he still presides over various Buddhist hells, which form
an elaborate complex in Buddhist mythology.

In the Buddhism of Tibet, Yama rules Naraka, the
region of torment. Each day Yama is forced to swallow
molten metal, since even Yama is finite. Yet he is also
judge and king of the dead. A person is judged solely on
his personal deeds, which are pictured as white pebbles on
a scale and weighed against his sins, which are black. The
person is dragged before Yama, who asks, "Did you not
when on earth see the five divine messengers sent to warn
you—the child, the old man, the sick, the criminal suffering punishment, and the dead corpse?"

"I did see them," the sinner replies.

"And did you not think within yourself, 'I am also subject to birth, old age, and death. Let me be careful to do
good works'?"

"I did not, sire," the man replies. "I neglected in my
folly to think of these things."

"These thine Evil deeds are not the work of thy mother,
father, relatives, friends, or foes. Thou alone hast done
them all," intones Yama. "Thou alone must gather the
fruit."

The convicted sinner is then taken by demons to the
place of torment. They rivet him to a red-hot iron, plunge
him in glowing seas of blood, and torture him on burning

coals until the last residue of his guilt has been expiated.

Hell is divided into numerous compartments, each with a special type of torture devised to suit the sins to be expiated. Only eight hells are mentioned in the early Buddhist books, but later tradition says there are eight hot hells and eight cold hells as well as an outer hell. These hells do not keep the sinner forever. After he suffers his full punishment, he is reborn.

If the person was Good and acted well, he is rewarded by a sojourn to the world of the gods. These heavens are arranged in stories, one above the other; the higher the heaven, the greater the perfection. But even heaven is not permanent and one must return to a lower life-form. The only true liberation comes when one attains Nirvana ("the blowing away," or "the extinguishing"). The term has baffled most Western commentators, some of whom have seen it only as a pessimistic notion of nonbeing, extinction, while others have tried to fit it into a Christian concept of heaven. Neither definition is correct according to D. T. Suzuki in his study *Outlines of Mahayana Buddhism.* Suzuki writes that Nirvana "is the annihilation of the notion of ego-substance and of all the desires that arise from this erroneous conception. But this represents the negative side of the doctrine, and its positive side consists in universal love or sympathy (*karuna*) for all beings. These two aspects of Nirvana (i.e., negatively, the destruction of evil passions, and positively, the practice of sympathy) are complementary to each other; and when we have one we have the other."

The entire Buddhist doctrine is summed up in *The Dhammapada:*

Some people are born again:
Evil-doers go to hell;
Righteous people go to heaven;
Those who are free from all worldly desires attain Nirvana.

Chapter 14

Chinese Mythology and Folklore

Yin and Yang express the concept of duality, yet gods and goddesses, such as Amit'o Fo and Kwan-yin, indicate the necessity for personal salvation.

Long ago in a small Chinese village a man and a dog died at the same time. One of the gods happened to pass by and saw the bodies of the two. He decided to bring them back to life. Looking first at the man, he saw that his body was whole except for the heart—it had rotted away. But the dog's heart was in fine condition, so the god placed the dog's heart in the man's body. He then made a heart from the mud nearby and placed it in the dog.

When he was finished, the god cast a magic spell over the bodies and they came to life. The dog wagged its tail in gratitude to the god. The man, however, did not thank the god, but cursed him.

This Chinese folktale, *Why Men Are So Bad*, displays one trait in Chinese folkbelief and philosophy—the inherent Evil of man. This position was summed up philosophically by Hsün Tzu, who lived in the third century BC. He wrote:

The nature of man is evil; his goodness is acquired. As to his nature, man is born, first, with a desire for gain. . . . Second, man is born with envy and hate. . . . Third, man is born with lusts of the ear and eye. . . . From all this, it is evident that the nature of man is evil and that his goodness is acquired.

The completely opposite stand was taken by Confucius (551–479 BC). He wrote, "The tendency of man's nature is good. There are none but have this tendency to good." The classic statement was given by Mencius (372–289 BC), a follower of Confucius. Mencius wrote:

It is by virtue of its innate quality that human nature can be considered good. This is why I say it is good. If it becomes evil, it is not the fault of its innate quality. The sense of compassion is common to all men; the sense of shame is common to all men; the sense of respect is common to all men; the sense of right and wrong is common to all men. . . . Humanity, righteousness, propriety, and wisdom are not taught; they are inherent in our nature.

The combination of the positive and negative beliefs regarding man's nature finds expression in the concept of Yin and Yang, symbolizing this conflict, which is necessary for all life. Yin and Yang are portrayed as a circle with curved dark and light halves. Yang, the light side, signifies Heaven, Sun, Light, Vigor, Male, Penetration. Yin, the dark side, symbolizes Earth, Moon, Darkness, Female, Absorption. In the Yin and Yang symbol, however, a portion of Yin is found in Yang and vice versa, again indicating the necessity of both in the creation and maintenance of life.

Yet the Yin and Yang concept seems to be later than a more primitive myth of creation, in which *Hun-tun* ("Chaos") is killed to create a structured world, since Chaos is Evil and Creation Good in all mythologies. Shû, the god of the Southern Ocean, and Hu, god of the Northern Ocean, were continually meeting in the land of Hun-tun. He treated them very well. One day they consulted together how they might repay his kindness.

"All men have seven orifices for the purpose of seeing, hearing, eating, and breathing," they said, "while this poor god, Hun-tun, has not one. Let us try and make them."

So Shû and Hu dug one orifice in Hun-tun every day for seven days. At the end of the seventh day Hun-tun died.

In Chinese, Shû-hu, the combining of the names of the two ocean gods, produces the word "lightning," which perhaps indicates the belief that lightning was responsible for ordering the mass of Chaos. In some texts Hun-tun is said to be a large yellow bird. It is interesting to note that in the Hebrew creation text in Genesis 1:2, God's spirit hovers above the waters like a bird.

In other Chinese texts a primeval being, P'an-ku, plays the part of creation, emerging from a Cosmic Egg which contains Yin and Yang. The heavy elements descend, producing the earth, while the lighter elements produce the sky. For 18,000 years P'an-ku grew at the rate of ten feet a day, filling the space between heaven and earth. When he died, his body became the natural elements making up the earth. In a variant myth, P'an-ku created the world, plants, and animals while still living. He then created people by first making figures out of clay. When they were dry, they were to be impregnated with the vital forces of Yin and Yang. Before full life came to them, a storm arose and P'an-ku pushed all the figurines, which were out to bake in the sun, into his house. Some of them were damaged, which is why some people are born lame or sick.

In his creation P'an-ku was aided by the Dragon, the Unicorn, the Tortoise, and the Phoenix, the four auspicious creatures. The Dragon is first because it is made of Yang; the Unicorn second because it has Yin and Yang; the Tortoise next because it possesses the secrets of life and death; and the Phoenix is included because its five colors blend, creating harmony. All of these are necessary for human life.

Man's soul, according to Chinese belief, is made up of Hun and P'o. Hun is Yang, pure and intelligent, and P'o is Yin, turbid and earthy. At birth they combine and at death they separate from one another, the P'o remaining near the burial chamber, while Hun is taken to Ti Yu ("the earth prison"). Ti Yu is the underworld in Chinese mythology, governed by the Shih-t'ien Yen-wang ("the Ten Kings"). Each rules over one of the hells, which are derived from Buddhist, Taoist, and native Chinese beliefs.

The ruler of the first hell is Ch'in-kuang-wang, who

meets the dead and examines their lives. Those whose sins and good works balance are sent back into the world to be born again. Those whose sins outweigh their good works are brought to the Sie-ching t'ai, a magic mirror which shows them all their victims and the sins they committed in life. After witnessing their lives, the sinners are taken to the other kings whose duty it is to judge and punish them. Suicides are sent back to earth as demons, since they have to live out their allotted time. On their return they are sent to Wang-si ch'eng ("city of the dead by accident"), from which no one ever comes back to be reborn.

The second hell is ruled by Ch'u-kiang wang, who punishes those dishonest male and female go-betweens in marriage, fraudulent trustees, ignorant doctors, and those who have wounded or mutilated persons or animals. This second hell is made up of sixteen smaller hells where the punishments are administered.

Sung-ti wang rules the third hell, which punishes unjust mandarins and all those who have behaved badly to their superiors, women who were shrews, slaves who injured their owners, cheating employees, condemned men who escaped from justice, and forgers, slanderers, and those who sold the family burial plot. As part of their punishment some of these sinners have their knees smashed, others their hearts and eyes pulled out.

The next hell, the fourth, is ruled by Wu-kuan wang. Here the rich who have never given alms, those who have sold medicine that does not cure, defrauders, makers of false weights and measures, and false traders, blasphemers, and those who steal from pagodas are punished. The damned are swept by a torrent, or they are set kneeling on sharpened bamboo, or they must remain sitting on spikes.

Yen Wang rules the fifth hell, where religious sins are punished, the sinners being those guilty of the death of living beings, incredulity, destruction of books of piety, or breaking their religious vows, as well as those guilty of lust, seduction, rape, and other sexual crimes. Yen Wang is derived from the Hindu god Yama. Yen Wang is often portrayed with Wu-Ch'ang Kuei, a man, and Yang Wu Ch'ang, a woman. The two are accompanied by Ma Mien ("horse face") and Niu T'ou ("ox head").

The sixth hell is ruled by Pien ch'eng. He punishes those guilty of sacrilege. The punishments consist of being crushed by a roller or sawed apart between two planks or flayed alive and stuffed. Some sinners are plunged into a pond of mud and human excrement; some are gnawed by rats or devoured by locusts; still others have burning torches thrust into their mouths.

T'ai-shan kun wang rules the seventh hell, where those who have violated graves or sold or eaten human flesh are punished. The sinners are plunged into vats of boiling oil or devoured by beasts such as dogs and pigs while demons pull out their intestines.

P'ing-Ten, ruler of the eighth hell, punishes those who have neglected family duty. They are crushed under chariot wheels, or their tongues are torn out. Some are plunged into latrines; others have nails driven into their heads; some are cut into little pieces.

The ninth hell is ruled by Tu-shi. Here incendiaries, abortionists, and obscene painters are punished. This hell is divided into sixteen smaller hells where the punishments are administered, such as being devoured by wasps, ants, scorpions, and serpents.

The tenth hell, ruled by Chuan-lun wang, does not administer punishment but arranges transmigrations after the soul's departure from hell. The ruler has eighty offices in which innumerable employees keep ledgers of reincarnations. Chuan-lun Wang pronounces whether the soul is to be reborn as human or animal, and what its degree of happiness will be. The soul is then taken to Men-p'o niang-niang, who concocts the Broth of Oblivion, which makes them forget the underworld. Once the bowl of broth is swallowed, the soul is led to K'u-ch'u k'iao ("the bridge of pain") which spans a river of crimson. Two demons ("Life is not long" and "Death is nigh") await the soul, which they plunge into the waters that carry it away to a new birth.

One Chinese folktale, *How Mu Lien Got His Mother out of Hell*, indicates the strength of hell's reality in Chinese Buddhist belief. Mu Lien was a Buddhist who lived during the Tang dynasty. He entered a monastery as a young man striving to become a Buddha ("Enlightened"). His mother, however, was Evil and envious. She wasted food by throwing it upon the floor. Whenever a beggar came to her house to ask for food, she ignored him. Eventually she died and was taken by two devils to the underworld.

She was sent to the hell of hunger where she was not given a grain to eat. Her tongue was tied down with an iron spike so that she could not utter a word. Whenever she cried out, all the hungry spirits cried out along with her. Two torches were lit in front of her eyes, so that she was blinded.

On earth Mu Lien had finally become a Buddha. He was granted permission to visit the underworld to bring his mother some rice. "She will want to eat," the demons warned Mu Lien, "but she will be unable to open her mouth." Nevertheless Mu Lien went to the hell of hunger.

The demons removed the spike from his mother's tongue and the torches from in front of her eyes. "I am very hungry," his mother said.

Mu Lien gave her the dish of rice, but she could not swallow the food since the fire inside her flashed out. The demons took Mu Lien's mother back to her prison cell.

Mu Lien became so angered that he struck the prison

door with his iron rod until it opened. Then he took his
mother up and carried her to heaven. But hundreds and
hundreds of demons also escaped and reached the earth.
When this was reported to the Lord of Heaven, he said:

"Mu Lien saved his mother, showing he has proper respect for his parent. She shall be pardoned. But he also let
loose a host of demons upon the world. He must recall
them back to hell where they belong. Only then will he be
readmitted to heaven."

Hundreds of years later a civil war broke out in which
thousands were killed. Mu Lien was reported to have been
seen during the battles. Those who died in the rebellion
were said to be the demons he had let loose.

The concept of hell in Chinese mythology is quite clear-
cut. The Chinese heaven into which Mu Lien's mother
was finally accepted is called either Ching T'u ("the Pure
Land") or Hsi fang chi-lo-shih-chieh ("the Paradise in the
West"). It is the goal of common people, displacing the
concept of Nirvana, which for many believers is a far too
philosophical concept. In the Pure Land sect of Chinese
Buddhism, heaven is ruled by Amit'o Fo, the Buddha of
Infinite Light. He is the personification of mercy, compassion, wisdom, and love, the supreme object of worship of
the Pure Land sect which developed in China, and also in
Japan, in reaction to the philosophically oriented Buddhism of the time.

Amit'o Fo is assisted in his work of salvation by Kwan-
yin ("she who always pays attention to sounds," i.e., hears
prayers). In both Chinese and Japanese Buddhism, she is
the goddess of mercy and patron of children. Originally
Kwan-yin was a male named Avalokitesvara. He was a
Bodhisattva, a Future Buddha, or one who has attained
Enlightenment and is entitled to enter Nirvana but re-
nounces it in order to teach mankind. During the Sung
Dynasty in China (960–1279), the male figure, Avalokites-

vara, was replaced as the female forms of the god appeared. According to one Chinese myth Kwan-yin was the daughter of an Indian prince. Her name was Miao Shan and she was a devoted follower of the Buddha.

In order to convert her blinded father to the light of Buddhism, Miao Shan visited him disguised as a stranger. She said that if he swallowed an eyeball of one of his children, he would have his sight restored. His children of course would not consent to what they considered madness. Miao Shan then miraculously created an eye which she fed to her father, restoring his sight. She convinced him to become a Buddhist by pointing out the folly of a world in which a child would not sacrifice his eye for a parent!

In another myth Kwan-yin was on her way to enter Nirvana when she paused on its threshold to listen to the cry of the world. She decided to stay in the world in order to teach mankind compassion and mercy.

Chapter 15

Japanese Mythology and Folklore

Amaterasu Omikami, the Shinto sun-goddess, battles
her brother Susano-o, the storm-god, portraying the
victory of light over the forces of chaos.

The Shinto deities Izanagi ("the male who invites") and Izanami ("the female who invites") looked down from the plain of heaven to the watery chaos below. Taking a jeweled spear, they stirred the waters, making larger and larger circles. When they drew up the spear, "the brine that dripped down from the end of the spear was piled up and became an island. This was the island of Onogoro."

Izanagi and Izanami then came down to the island but found it was deserted. They were lonely, and after looking intently at one another for some time, they decided to marry. "How is thy body formed?" Izanagi asked Izanami.

"My body is completely formed except for one part which is incomplete," she replied.

"My body is completely formed and there is one part which is superfluous. Suppose that we supplement that which is incomplete in thee with that which is superfluous in me, and thereby procreate lands."

Izanagi and Izanami then had sexual relations from which a child was born, but it had no legs, so it was cast adrift in a reed boat. Their second child was the Island Awa, but they also refused it. Izanagi and Izanami returned to heaven to ask the other gods for help to discover the cause of their difficulties. They were told that when they made love, Izanami spoke first—which was wrong. The man was to speak first. (Thus at a Shinto wedding ceremony the groom speaks first.) When they next had a child, Izanami gave birth to the Eight Islands which became Japan. The heavenly couple continued producing islands and gods until Izanami died while giving birth to the fire-god.

Izanagi descended to the underworld in search of his dead wife, but when he found only the decaying corpse, he fled in horror. Reaching the upper earth again, he hastened to bathe and purify himself in the river. From every garment he threw off, and from every part of his body, was born a fresh god. Among them, the sun-goddess, Amaterasu Omikami ("heaven-shining great goddess"), came from his left eye, and her brother the storm-god, Susano-o ("swift impetuous male"), came from his nose.

The sun-goddess, Amaterasu, taught her people to plant rice and weave cloth. Her brother Susano-o one day asked his father, Izanagi, for permission to visit his sister. When Susano-o arrived at her dwelling, he caused great havoc, committing obscene acts which, according to the *Kojiki* ("Records of Ancient Matters," written in the eighth century), "so greatly mortified his august sister Amaterasu Omikami, that she hid herself in a cave, whereupon both heaven and earth became dark. To entice her forth, the eight million spirits of the Plain of Heaven assembled before the cave many trees bedecked with jewels, lit bonfires, and laughed aloud with such uproar at a raucous dance performed by a spirit-female named Uzume that the goddess in her cave, becoming curious, opened the door to peek out. They held a mirror before her, the first she had ever seen: She was drawn out, and the world again was alight."

After the world was restored to light, Susano-o was exiled and fled to the earth, to Izumo (Japan). His descendants gradually took possession of the land that had given them hospitality. Later the grandson of Amaterasu, called Ninigi no Mikoto, came in person to rule the land and married the goddess of Mount Fuji. Ninigi was the great-grandfather of Jimmu Tenno, the first historical Emperor of Japan, creating the line from which the Japanese imperial house claims Amaterasu as its divine ancestor.

Though Susano-o's attempted destruction of his sister's realm places him among the malevolent forces in mythology, his character displays more the nature of a Trickster than a demon. (A Trickster acts without regard to moral consequences, rather in the nature of Bugs Bunny, for example, in modern folklore.)

One myth also contained in the *Kojiki* tells of Susano-o's subsequent fate after being exiled. Susano-o arrived at the river Hi in Izumo. He saw at that time some chopsticks floating down the stream, and he thought, therefore, that there must be people above. Proceeding upward in quest of them, he discovered an old man and woman, with a young girl between them; they were crying.

"I am an Earth Spirit," the old man said, "and my name is Foot-Stroking Elder. My wife's name is Hand-Stroking Elder. And this our daughter's name is Mistress Head Comb."

Susano-o then asked, "And what is the cause of your weeping?"

"Once we had eight daughters," the old man said, "but there is an eight-forked serpent that comes each year and eats one. His time has come round again. That is why we weep."

"What is the serpent's form?" Susano-o asked.

"The eyes are as red as the winter cherry. It has one body with eight heads and tails. On that body moss grows, and conifers; the length extends over eight valleys and eight hills, and if one looks at the belly, it is constantly bloody and inflamed."

Then looking at the girl, Susano-o asked, "This being your daughter, will you give her to me?"

The old man replied, "With reverence. However, I do not know your name."

"I am the elder brother of the goddess Amaterasu, and am descended here from heaven."

"That being so, with reverence, she is yours," the old man replied. Then Susano-o took the girl at once, changed her into a multitudinously close-toothed comb, and placed it in his hair.

"Distill a brew of eightfold refined liquor," he told the couple. "Also, make a fence round about, and in that fence let there be eight gates; at each gate let there be eight platforms; and on each platform a liquor vat, into each of which pour the eightfold liquor; and wait."

They did as they were told. The eight-forked serpent came at the appointed time and dipped a head into each vat. Then, having become drunk, every one of its heads lay down to sleep. Susano-o drew his ten-grasp sword and cut the monster into pieces.

Susano-o's destruction of the eight-forked dragon is one of the many Japanese tales which contain a battle between Good and Evil. Perhaps the best known of such tales is this one of the hero Momotaro:

One day the wife of a poor woodcutter went to the river to wash some clothes. As she was about to return, she saw a large object floating in the water. She pulled it close to land and saw that it was a large peach, larger than any she had ever seen. She took it home, washed it, and handed it to her husband to open. As the man cut it, a boy emerged from the kernel. They adopted him as a present from the gods to comfort them in their old age. They called the boy Momotaro ("the elder son of the peach"), and he grew up big and strong, excelling the other boys his own age. One day Momotaro decided to leave his foster parents and go to Onigashima ("the Island of Devils") to seek his fortune. The foster parents gave him some dumplings to carry with him.

Momotaro soon met a dog, who asked for a dumpling and promised to accompany him. Then a monkey and a pheasant came with similar requests. With his three companions Momotaro reached the devils' fortress. He had a battle with the demons in which he was helped by the animals. Finally they reached the inner part of the fortress, where the chief devil, Akandoji, was waiting for them with an iron war club. He was thrown down by

Momotaro, who bound him with ropes and made him disclose the secret of his treasures. Then Momotaro helped himself to Akandoji's trove and left with his three companions for home, where he became a rich and honored member of the community.

While the myth of Susano-o and the tale of Momotaro contain in strong outline the conflict between the forces of Good and Evil, many other Japanese tales dwell on the demonic for sheer pleasure. So strong in fact was the belief in demonic spirits and ghosts in Japan that the government in 1808 legislated against certain ghost stories, in the hope that people would cease reading them. It took television, however, to accomplish that, though Japanese movies often dwell on fantasy-horror motifs.

Among some of the more popular ghosts, demons, and gods in Japanese folkore are Oiwa, Ubume, Yuki Onna, and Kishimojin. Oiwa was the ghost of a woman killed by her husband. She came back to haunt him sometimes in the form of a long-tailed ghost, other times as a mutilated woman. By her frequent visitations she frightened her husband into remorse and repentance for her murder. Finally he went insane and died.

Ubume is the Evil spirit of an old woman of the underworld. She appears with a child in her arms and asks a passerby to hold the infant, then she goes off. The weight of the child increases by degrees until it drops to the ground in the shape of a huge boulder.

Yuki Onna ("snow woman") is a ghost who appears in snowstorms, causing travelers to fall asleep and thereby freeze to death.

Kishimojin, the last of this small sampling, represents a case of a demoness transformed into a beneficent goddess. Originally Kishimojin was a cannibal woman in Hindu mythology whose legend was brought to Japan with the arrival of Buddhism. In one account she was condemned to give birth to five hundred children to pay for her Evil deeds, earning for herself the title Mother of Demons. In a variant of the myth she was sent to hell and reborn in the shape of a ghoul to give birth to five hundred devils, of which she was to eat one a day, since she had sworn in her life to devour all the children in one village.

In both these myths one of her children, Bingara, is converted by the Buddha, and later Kishimojin is also converted. She is now worshiped in Japan as the goddess of women in childbirth, prayed to for offspring, and viewed as protector of the Buddhist world and of children in particular.

Not only does Good conquer Evil in Japanese folklore, but Evil is also transformed into Good.

Chapter 16

African Mythologies and Folklores

Myths and folktales of the origin of life and death
display the contrast between Good and Evil in Africa.

The Dahomean of Africa tell how God and his son Legba once lived on earth at the beginning of time. Legba did only what God told him to do, but the people blamed Legba when Evil occurred. God was always credited with all the Good that happened. Legba felt that this was unfair. Why should only he be blamed when God was responsible? But when he complained of this to God, he was told that this was the way it was to be. One day Legba tried to trick God, stealing yams from God's garden while wearing God's sandals. When a search for the thief was conducted, Legba suggested that God must have taken the yams in his sleep. God knew that Legba was trying to deceive him.

In anger God left the earth and returned to the sky, telling Legba to visit him at night and describe what happened during the day. In a variant of this myth Legba told an old woman to throw her dirty wash water into the sky. This act so angered God that he went up to the sky, leaving Legba to control the earth.

In both myths the central concept is that the creator sky-god leaves the domain of the earth and its running to a lesser being. God becomes tired, exhausted, or bored in many African myths, removing himself from the world. Lesser deities, many of whom do not live up to God's high moral standards, are then made custodians of the earth. But God is so removed from man that man finds he must deal with God's underlings, such as Legba. Many rites are thus associated with placating Legba.

Legba's importance is reflected in the fact that his worship is also found among the blacks of Dutch Guiana, Brazil, Trinidad, Cuba, and in the Voudun, or Voodoo, cult in New Orleans and on the island of Hispaniola.

In Haitian Voodoo worship, Legba is a "principle of life." His symbol indicates both masculine and feminine attributes, making him a sign of totality. Legba is guardian of the sacred gateway, the Grand Chemin, the road that leads from the finite world to the spiritual one. In rites he is often addressed, "Papa Legba, open the gate . . . open the gates so that we may pass through."

Some Voodoo sects believe that Legba was Jesus. Legba was hung on a cross, they contend, to serve as edible human sacrifice—which, they point out, is what is meant by the words used in the Christian rite of Holy Eucharist: "This is my Body. . . . This is my Blood." Christian priests on the island of Haiti, however, equate Legba with the Devil, since his actions make him fit neatly into this Christian concept.

The myth of Legba and God is not as dualistic as that of the Edo-speaking peoples of Benin, a province of Southern Nigeria. According to one myth, Osa, the sky-god who lives in the heavens, created the world, while his Evil counterpart Osanoha ("Osa of the bush") created a house of sickness in which diseases live. When men and women on their way from heaven to earth came near the house, rain fell and drove them into it for shelter. Thus sickness came to earth. Because of the wickedness of Osanoha, who also created animals, men and animals are enemies and hunt one another.

In a variant myth Osa and Osanoha agreed to reckon up and compare their riches. Osa had more children than Osanoha, and the two have been enemies ever since, contending for the hearts of men, one doing Good, the other Evil.

A myth of the people of Ghana tells that God had two sons, Tano and Bia. The older son, Bia, was the more obedient. God wanted to give him the fertile lands of the earth to control. Tano was to receive the barren lands. However, a goat told Tano of God's plan. So Tano disguised himself as Bia and arrived at God's house before

Bia had a chance to get there. God mistakenly gave the fertile land to Tano, a decision he could not revoke. This tale is similar to that of Esau and Jacob in the Old Testament (Genesis 27), in which Jacob tricks his father Abraham to win the older Esau's birthright.

Tano is looked upon not only as a river-god but also as the god who in some way helped oppose Death, the origin of which forms one of the main motifs in African mythology.

Once a hunter hit an antelope with his arrow, and the animal was transformed into the god Tano. He quelled the hunter's fears, offering to protect him. As they traveled together, they came upon Death. Death was opposed to Tano's being a companion of man, and Tano, being a strong-willed god, was angry at Death's interference in the matter. To settle the disagreement, the two began a singing contest—taunting each other with songs. At last they agreed that when a person became ill, the outcome of the illness would depend upon which of the two reached him first. If Tano arrived first, the man would live, but if it were Death, he would die.

In Angola the Mbundu tell of King Kitamba, who was very saddened by the death of his first wife. He insisted that all his subjects join him in a state of perpetual mourning. No one was permitted to speak or make any other noises in public. Despite the fact that the lesser chiefs objected strenuously to the proclamation, Kitamba bade the mourning period continue. A council of elders appointed a doctor to help in the matter. The doctor and his little son entered a grave which had been dug in the floor of their home in their effort to reach the underworld. Each day the doctor's wife did as she was directed and, dressed in mourning, poured water onto the gravesite. At last the doctor and his son came upon the king's dead wife, who explained to them that no one once dead could return to the realm of the living. She gave the doctor her armlet so that Kitamba would know that the doctor had succeeded in reaching her. When Kitamba saw the armlet he finally permitted the mourning to end.

In central Africa the name *Leza* is used by a number of peoples to refer to God. The Ila of Zambia tell how God Leza ("the one who besets") caused the brothers, sisters, and parents of a small girl from a large family to die. In time all her other relatives died. Left an orphan, she eventually married and had children, but before very long her husband died. After her children gave birth to their children, they too were taken by Leza. Leza even caused the aging woman's grandchildren not to live long. To her great surprise, however, each day the woman seemed to grow younger instead of older. She decided to build a ladder to heaven to ask God Leza why he was doing these things, but the ladder crumbled before she could reach the sky. So she tried to find a road that would lead to God. She asked everyone she met where the road might be, and told her sad story to all the people she spoke to along the way. They explained to her that all people were put into the world to suffer and that she was no exception. The woman never did find the road leading to God and eventually, like all human beings, died.

The Buganda of Uganda refer to Kaizuki as the brother of Death. They claim that Death apparently did not want Kintu and Nambi, the first man and woman, to leave heaven for earth. Gulu, the father of Nambi, and god of the sky, warned them of Death's desire, suggesting that they leave as soon as possible and not return for anything. Nambi, despite her husband's warning against it, returned to heaven to ask her father, Gulu, for grain to feed her fowl. She and her husband had left heaven with cows, a banana tree, and sheep, goat, and fowl.

Nambi's brother, Death, took this opportunity to follow

his sister to earth. Kintu became very angry at this, but his wife told him to be patient and see if anything bad would happen. For a while both Kintu and Nambi lived very happily. They had many children. Eventually Death came to their home and asked for one of Kintu's children to serve as his cook. After being turned down, Death asked for the second time, but still Kintu refused on the basis that Gulu would not be pleased to see his grandson working as Death's cook. Death then threatened to kill the child if Kintu would not agree to give him up.

When Kintu did not agree, the child died. In time more of Kintu's children died, and so he returned to Gulu to find out what if anything could be done to stop Death. Gulu reminded Kintu of the warning that Gulu had given Kintu and Nambi, but in the end Gulu sent Kaizuki, the brother of both Nambi and Death, to assist the family. Kaizuki had a fight with Death but could not overcome him. The second attempt was equally unsuccessful, for after Kaizuki lured Death out of his hiding place in the ground, some children came along and aroused his fear of attack. Kaizuki could not get to him and eventually tired of the pursuit. Since then Death, who lives in the ground, is always present.

The Mbundu of Angola tell of Ngunza, who was one of two brothers. He dreamed that his brother died while Ngunza was on a trip away from home. When he returned, his mother explained that Death was the cause, and so Ngunza set a large trap to capture Death. When Death was caught, he begged to be set free, arguing that he was not responsible for killing people. He said that it was invariably the fault of some human being, often of the victim himself. They set off together to visit the Land of Death so that Ngunza could see this for himself. He did in fact come to realize that what Death had said was true. Ngunza found his brother living very well, better in fact than he had lived when he was on earth. Ngunza returned home and was given the seeds of all the significant plants that grow in Angola. In time Death came looking for him, but Ngunza resented the persistent way in which he was pursued. Finally Death threw an ax at Ngunza, who quickly turned into a spirit.

Another African myth tells of a different origin of death. Once upon a time men sent a dog with a message to the god Uwolowu to say that when they died, they would like to come to life again. So off the dog trotted to deliver the message. But on the way the dog felt hungry and turned in at a house where a man was boiling magic herbs. The dog sat down and thought to himself, "He is cooking food." Meantime a frog had set out to tell Uwolowu that when men died, they would rather *not* come to life again. Nobody had asked the frog to take that message; he made up the lie.

The dog, who still sat hopefully watching the man cook, saw the frog racing by, but said to himself, "When I have had a snack, I'll catch up with froggy." However, the frog arrived first and said to Uwolowu, "When men die, they would rather not come to life again." After Uwolowu heard that message, the dog entered and announced, "When men die, they would like to come to life again." Uwolowu was puzzled and said to the dog, "I really don't understand these two messages. As I heard the frog's message first, I will comply with it. I will not do what you have asked." That is the reason why death is in the world.

With so much of its mythology concerned with the origin of death, it is not strange to understand that magic and sorcery play an important part in African beliefs, since material and spiritual matters are frequently indistinguishable. Many villages in West Africa, for example, are entered through a protecting arch which is supposed to remove Evil. It is believed that Evil spirits will follow the road and try to enter the village if not prevented.

The use of medicines made by a traditional medicine

man are an important part of the community tradition. The Evil counterpart, the "black magician," works harm and is feared and hated.

The dead and their ghosts also play an important part in African belief. The soul is believed to leave the body at the last breath, or when the body is placed in the earth. It may (as in ancient Egyptian belief and Medieval Christian lore) hover around the body for some days, or be available to receive gifts. The dead go to a world that is dark and cold, under the earth, similar to the Hades of the Greeks, and the Sheol of the ancient Hebrews. Some Africans, however, perhaps under Christian influence, believe that the Good go to a heaven of "fresh breezes" and the Evil to a "heaven of broken pots."

Chapter 17

North American Indian Mythologies

Duality portrayed in the conflict between brothers and the amoral Trickster knowing neither Good nor Evil give us a mirror by which to see ourselves.

Long ago there grew a stately tree that branched beyond the range of vision. Perpetually laden with fruit and blossoms, it made the air fragrant with its perfume. People gathered to its shade when councils were held. One day the Great Ruler said to his people, "We will make a new place where another people may grow. Under our council tree is a great cloud sea which calls for our help. It is lonesome. It knows no rest and calls for light. We will talk to it. The roots of our council tree point to it and will show the way."

Having commanded that the tree be uprooted, the Great Ruler peered into the depths where the roots had been. He then summoned Ata-en-sic, the sky-woman, who was with child, and asked her to look down. She saw nothing. The Great Ruler, however, knew that the sea voice was calling, and he wrapped around Ata-en-sic a great ray of light and sent her down to the cloud sea.

When the animals saw the blinding light, they became frightened. "If it falls, we will be destroyed," they cried out.

"Where can it rest?" asked Duck.

"Only the *oeh-da* ("earth") can hold it," said Beaver, "the *oeh-da* which lies at the bottom of our waters. I will bring it up."

Beaver went down but never returned. Then Duck ventured, but soon his dead body floated to the surface. Many other divers also failed. Then Muskrat, knowing the way, volunteered. He soon returned, bearing a small portion of mud in his paw.

"It is heavy and will grow fast," he said. "But who will bear its weight?"

Turtle was willing, and *oeh-da* was placed on his hard shell. Hah-nu-nah, Turtle, then became the Earth Bearer.

The *oeh-da* grew and Ata-en-sic, hearing the voices under her heart, one soft and soothing, the other loud and contentious, knew that her mission to people island was nearing.

Inside Ata-en-sic were Do-ya-da-no, the twin brothers. One, Hah-gweh-di-yu, was Good. The other, Hah-gweh-da-et-gah, was Evil. Discovering that there was some light under his mother's armpit, Hah-gweh-da-et-gah thrust himself through it, causing Ata-en-sic's death. The Good brother, however, was born in the natural manner. Foreknowing their powers, each claimed dominion over the other. Hah-gweh-di-yu claimed the right to beautify the land, while Hah-gweh-da-et-gah was determined to destroy it.

Hah-gweh-di-yu shaped the sky with the palm of his hand, and created the sun from the face of his dead mother, saying, "You shall rule here where your face will shine forever."

But the Evil Hah-gweh-da-et-gah set darkness in the western sky, to drive the sun down before it.

Hah-gweh-di-yu, the Good, then drew forth from the breast of his mother the moon and the stars and led them to the sun as his sisters who would guard his night sky. He gave to the earth her body, its Great Mother, from whom was to spring all life.

The twins then created what is upon the earth. Hah-gweh-di-yu created mountains, valleys, forests, fruit-bearing trees, and good animals such as the deer. Hah-gweh-da-et-gah, the Evil One, created monsters that dwell in the sea, hurricanes, tempests, wild beasts that devour, grim flying creatures that steal life without sign, and creeping reptiles that poison.

When the earth was completed, Hah-gweh-di-yu bestowed a protecting Spirit upon each of his creations. He then asked Hah-gweh-da-et-gah to make peace, but the

Evil One refused and challenged the Good One to combat—the victor to be ruler of the earth.

Hah-gweh-da-et-gah proposed weapons which he could control: poisonous roots strong as flint, monsters' teeth, and fangs of serpents. But these Hah-gweh-di-yu refused, selecting instead the thorns of the giant crabapple tree, which were arrow-pointed and strong.

They fought with the thorns, and Hah-gweh-da-et-gah was defeated. The Good One, having become ruler of the earth, banished his brother to a pit under the earth from which he cannot return. But the Evil One still retains Servers, half-human, half-beast, whom he sends to continue his destructive work. They can assume any form. The Good Hah-gweh-di-yu is continually creating and protecting.

This Iroquois Indian myth displays a dualistic concept of Good and Evil, neatly matching other mythologies, such as Persian, where Good and Evil are embodied in two divinities, Ahura Mazda and Ahriman. Other American Indian myths stress the same motif, such as the Algonquin myth of Gluskap,, the culture hero who kills his Evil brother Malsum. At the end of that tale Malsum is placed underground, and Gluskap creates the world from the body of their dead mother, who died at the birth of Malsum.

The Senecas have a similar myth of twins, one called Othagwenda ("Flint") of a reddish color, and the other, Djuskaha ("Little Sprout"), who was light in color. In this myth Othagwenda goes westward and Djuskaha eastward. In time they return to see what the other has created on earth. Othagwenda creates rocky terrain and a gigantic mosquito, while Djuskaha made the sycamore tree to bear Good fruit and formed rivers so that half the water flowed upstream and the other half down. Othagwenda was not pleased with his brother's creations, saying that people who were to come into this world would find it too easy. A fight ensued and Othagwenda was killed.

These North American Indian myths are open to some suspicion, since they have all been recorded by white Christian settlers. Just how much Christian veneer is placed over them? The Iroquois Seneca myth of Othagwenda and Djuskaha was first recorded by Jesuit missionaries in the seventeenth century. Even if the myth continues to be part of an oral tradition today, it is unlikely that the Indian legend has not been influenced by the white man's Christian concepts.

This question is raised since the mass of American Indian legends do not display a dualistic concept of Good and Evil. In *The Report on the Indian Tribes*, compiled by Whipple in 1855, the author writes that the Cherokees "know nothing of the Evil One and his domains, except what they have learned from white men."

In *The Myths of the New World* (1896), Daniel G. Brinton wrote that "moral dualism can only arise where the ideas of good and evil are not synonymous with those of pleasure and pain, for the conception of a wholly good or a wholly evil nature requires the use of these terms in their higher ethical senses. The various deities of the Indians . . . present no stronger antithesis in this respect than those of ancient Greece or Rome. Some gods favored man and others hurt him; some, like the forces they embodied, were beneficent to him, others injurious. But no ethical contrast, beyond what this would imply, existed to the native mind."

Brinton's contention, though made nearly a hundred years ago, is supported by one present-day Arapaho Indian, Richard Pratt. In *American Indian Mythology* (1968), a collection of myths recently recorded, Pratt says, "All that talk about the Great Spirit and Happy Hunting Ground is a cliché and they've worn it out. The old people didn't think like that. . . . . There is no difference in the afterlife between the good and the bad; all share the same world after death. It is the Arapaho way not to judge people."

This Indian statement stems from one of the basic motifs encountered in their beliefs—power has no "morality" attached to it. The same power that produces Good also produces Evil. Various gods and spirits hold power. Evil is not intrinsic to one particular god.

This concept leaves open the question of suffering, sickness, and death. How did these come about? One Navaho myth attempts to give an explanation.

The Twin Warrior Gods were sent by the Turquoise Woman to destroy Disease, Hunger, Old Age, and Poverty—each of which was embodied in a husband-and-wife pair. As the Twin Gods approached, the couples warned that without Disease, one would not know health; without Hunger, the joy of eating; without Old Age, the joy of youth; and without Poverty, people would become lazy and not work.

While this explanation leaves much to be desired as an answer to the question of the necessity of Evil, one point becomes clear in Indian belief: There is no concept of "sin" as in Jewish or Christian beliefs. Disease, hunger, and poverty come about because of the natural order, not because mankind in some way has broken its covenant with God.

The complete absence of "sin" or any consciousness of it is found in the character of the Trickster. We earlier met the Greek Trickster Prometheus and the Nordic one, Loki. His American Indian counterpart, however, best embodies the concept. Paul Radin made a study of this in his book, *The Trickster* (1956), and writes, "Trickster is at one and the same time creator and destroyer, giver and negator, he who dupes others and who is always duped himself. He wills nothing consciously. At all times he is constrained to behave as he does from impulses over

which he has no control. He knows neither good nor evil
yet he is responsible for both. He possesses no values,
moral or social, is at the mercy of his passions and appe-
tites, yet through his actions all values come into being."

Often Trickster is identified with animals, such as
Raven, Coyote, Hare, or Spider. In the Winnebago cycle
collected by Radin in his book, Trickster does not possess
any definite shape, but rather a form approximating
human shape. Trickster has a sexual appetite that is enor-
mous.

In Episode 16 (of the cycle of 49), Trickster sees some
women swimming, the chief's daughter among them. He
takes his penis out of a box (he carries it on his back) and
places it in the water, telling it to "lodge squarely" in the
chief's daughter. The penis slides along the water and
achieves its target. The women, and then the men, try to
pull it out, but to no avail. They then call an old woman
to give them advice; she answers that Trickster is having
intercourse, and their efforts are all annoying him. The
old woman then sings and the penis "is jerked out."
Trickster becomes upset, saying, "Why is she doing this
when I am trying to have intercourse? Now she has
spoiled all the pleasure!"

Other episodes in the cycle tell how Trickster was
changed into a woman (#20); falls into his own excrement
(#24); eats children (#27); lures a bear to its death (#35);
is outwitted by Mink, who gets bear meat (#36); discards
pieces of penis and throws them into a lake where they
become plants (#39); and eats a final meal on earth and returns to heaven (#49).

What does this seemingly meaningless array of antics
signify? Commenting on the character, Carl Jung wrote:

The Trickster is a primitive "cosmic" being of *divine-animal*
nature, on the one hand superior to man because of his superhu-
man qualities, and on the other hand inferior to him because of

his unreason and unconsciousness. He is no match for the animals either, because of his extraordinary clumsiness and lack of instinct. These defects are the marks of his *human* nature, which is not so well adapted to the environment as the animals' but, instead, has prospects of a much higher development of consciousness based on considerable eagerness to learn.

Trickster lives on today not only in American Indian mythology but also in such cartoon characters as Bugs Bunny, Daffy Duck, and various other comic figures who are often the butt of their own pranks. Why does the character continue to survive through various transformations? The answer may lie in the fact that all of us, no matter how "highly developed" or civilized, have Trickster as part of our makeup. We live the Trickster life often in our dreams and fantasies, where we can do what we will without punishment, and also in our myths, where the Evil is deflected from our moral consciousness: We didn't do it— Trickster did.

Chapter 18

Aztec, Mayan, and Inca Mythologies

Conflict and resolution appear in the myths of
Quetzalcoatl, Tezcatlipoca, and Coatlicue, and the
conflict between life and death in Mayan myths,
while the Inca creator-god, Viracocha, demands blood
sacrifice to satisfy his hunger.

Ometecuhtli ("the lord of duality") was the ancient Aztec supreme being who existed outside space and time. He was the source of all life. According to C. A. Burland, in his study *The Gods of Mexico* (1967), the ancient Mexicans "were quite sure that in everything there was a unity of opposing factors, of male and female, of light and dark, of movement and stillness, of order and disorder. This opposition and duality was an essential of everything, and they felt that it was through this principle that life came into being."

Ometecuhtli, however, was too far removed from the everyday aspect of life for the Mexicans. Other gods, both Good and Evil, filled the natives' pantheon. One of the most important was Quetzalcoatl, whose name has been interpreted as "feathered serpent," "precious twin," and "precious serpent." Actually there are two Quetzalcoatls, one the wind-god, the other a culture-hero. Often the two are combined into one being in various accounts.

In his purely mythical form Quetzalcoatl was one of four brothers born in the thirteenth heaven. Two were called the black and red Tezcatlipoca, and the fourth was Huitzilopochtli. Tezcatlipoca (the black and red are blended into one god in the myths) was the wisest. He knew all thoughts and could see into the future. At a certain time the four brothers had gathered together and consulted concerning the creation of things. The work was left to Quetzalcoatl and Huitzilopochtli. First they made fire, then half a sun, the heavens, the waters, and a great fish called Cipactli, and from its flesh the solid earth.

The first couple were the man Cipactonal and the woman Oxomuco. They had a son, but there was no wife for him to marry, so the four gods made one for him out of the hair taken from the head of their divine mother, Xochiquetzal.

The half sun created by Quetzalcoatl was a poor light for the world, and the four came together again to find a means of adding another half to it. Not waiting for their decision, Tezcatlipoca transformed himself into a sun. The other brothers then filled the world with giants, who tore up the trees with their hands. After some time Quetzalcoatl took a stick and "with a blow of it knocked Tezcatlipoca from the sky into the waters." Quetzalcoatl then made himself into the sun. Tezcatlipoca transformed himself into a tiger and emerged from the waves, attacking and devouring the giants, and then passing to the "nocturnal heavens," he became the constellation Great Bear.

As the sun Quetzalcoatl made the earth flourish, but Tezcatlipoca was merely biding his time. When the right moment appeared, in his tiger form he gave Quetzalcoatl such a blow with his paw that it hurled him from the skies. Quetzalcoatl then swept the earth with a violent tornado that destroyed all the inhabitants except for a few "who were changed into monkeys." Then when Tezcatlipoca placed Tlaloc, the rain-god, as the sun in the heavens, Quetzalcoatl "poured a flood of fire upon the earth, drove Tlaloc from the sky, and placed in his stead, as sun, the goddess Chalchiutlicue, the Emerald Skirted, wife of Tlaloc." When she ruled as the sun, the earth was flooded and all humans were drowned again except for those who were changed into fishes. As a result, "the heavens themselves fell, and the sun and stars were alike quenched."

The two then realized that their struggle had to end, so they united "their efforts and raised again the sky, resting it on two mighty trees, tezcaquahuitl ("tree of the mirror") and quetzalveixochitl ("beautiful great rose tree"), on which the concave heavens have ever since securely rested.

The earth still had no sun to light it, and the four brothers met again. They decided to make a sun, one that would "eat the hearts and drink the blood of victims, and there must be wars upon the earth, that these victims could be obtained for the sacrifice." Quetzalcoatl then built a great fire and took his son, born of his own flesh without any mother, and cast him into the flames "whence he rose into the sky as the sun which lights the world." Tlaloc then threw his son into the flames, and the moon arose.

The Quetzalcoatl of the above myth is a god. The Quetzalcoatl of another Aztec myth is not a god, but a culture-hero, a high priest of the city of Tula. He was the teacher of arts, the wise lawgiver, the virtuous prince, the master-builder, and the merciful judge. He lived a life of fasting and prayer.

The hero (as opposed to the god) Quetzalcoatl either came as a stranger to the Aztecs from an unknown land or was born in Tula where he reigned as priest-king. For many years he ruled the city and at last began to build a very great temple. While engaged in its construction, Tezcatlipoca (who in other myths is a creator-Trickster god, but here is a demonic force or sorcerer) came to Quetzalcoatl one day and told him that toward Honduras, in a place called Tlapallan, a house was ready for him. He should leave Tula and go to live and die in the new home.

Quetzalcoatl said that the heavens and the stars had already warned him that after four years he must leave, and he would therefore obey. He left with all the inhabitants of Tula. Some he left in Cholula, from whom its descendants come, and others in Cempoal. At last he reached Tlapallan, and on the same day that he arrived he fell sick and died.

There is another, better-known account in the *Annals of Cuauhtitlan*. When those opposed to Quetzalcoatl did not succeed in their designs to rid themselves of his presence, they summoned Tezcatlipoca, who said, "We will give him a drink to dull his reason, and will show him his own face in a mirror, and surely he will be lost."

Then Tezcatlipoca brewed an intoxicating drink, *pulque*, and taking a mirror, he wrapped it in a rabbit skin and went to the house of Quetzalcoatl.

"Go tell your master," he said to the servants, "that I have come to show him his own flesh."

"What is this?" asked Quetzalcoatl when the message was delivered. "What does he call my own flesh? Go and ask him." Tezcatlipoca said he would speak only with Quetzalcoatl. He was then admitted into the presence of Quetzalcoatl.

"Welcome, youth. You have troubled yourself much. Whence come you? What is this, my flesh, that you would show me?"

"My Lord and Priest," replied Tezcatlipoca, "I come from the mountainside of Nonoalco. Look now at your flesh; know yourself; see yourself as you are seen by others." And with that he handed him the mirror.

As soon as Quetzalcoatl saw his face in the mirror, he said, "How is it possible my subjects can look on me without fright? Well might they flee from me. How can a man remain among them filled as I am with foul sores? I shall be seen no more; I shall no longer frighten my people."

But Tezcatlipoca said he could conceal the defects on Quetzalcoatl's face. He painted the ruler's cheeks green and dyed his lips red. He colored the forehead yellow, and taking the feathers of the *quechol* bird, he made a beard. Quetzalcoatl looked at himself in the mirror and was pleased with the artifice.

Then Tezcatlipoca took the strong *pulque* which he had brewed and gave some to Quetzalcoatl, who became drunk. He called his attendants and asked that his sister, Quetzalpetlatl, come to him. She obeyed instantly and also became drunk.

In this myth, it is not clear whether Quetzalcoatl slept with his sister, but the next morning, he said, "I have sinned, the stain on my name can never be erased. I am not fit to rule this people. Let them build for me a habitation deep under ground; let them bury my bright treasures in the earth; let them throw the gleaming gold and shining stone into the holy fountain where I take my daily bath."

He then journeyed eastward to a place where the sky, land, and water meet. There his attendants built a funeral pyre and he threw himself into the flames. As his body burned, his heart rose to heaven, and after four days he became the planet Venus, the Morning Star.

In a variant of the end of this legend, Quetzalcoatl departed on a raft toward the east, saying he would one day return. When Hernando Cortes (1485–1547) and the Spaniards were first spotted by the Aztecs, the natives believed that their hero had returned to them as he had promised— a belief which helped seal their doom. The conflict between the two cultures is told in W. H. Prescott's *The Conquest of Mexico* (1843) and in the novels *The Fair God* (1873) by Lew Wallace and *Captain from Castile* (1945) by Samuel Shellambarger, which was made into a film (1947).

No movies to my knowledge have been made about Coatlicue ("the serpent lady," or "robe of the serpent"), though she figures as the great mother-goddess among the Aztecs, combining both beneficent and demonic roles.

According to Fray Bernardino Sahagún in his *Historia General de las Cosas de Nueva España* (1570–1582), Coatlicue was responsible for giving people "poverty, mental depression, and sorrows." She would often appear in the marketplace dressed as a lady of rank and leave a cradle in which was found a lance point later used in human sacrifices to the gods.

Fray Diego Durán in *Historia de las Indias de Nueva España e Islas de Tierra Firme* (1580–1581) relates that Montezuma II sent representatives to find the origin of his ancestors. They discovered a hill containing seven caves. An

Indian priest appeared who introduced them to an old woman, ugly and dirty, whose "face was so black and covered with filth that she looked like something straight out of Hell." She welcomed the ambassadors and said she was the mother of the god Huitzilopochtli. She had been fasting since the day he left, not washing or combing her hair, but waiting for his return from the Aztec land. As the messengers prepared to leave she called to them, telling them that in her land no one grew old.

The old woman then told them to watch one of her servants run down a hill and become younger as he reached bottom. The ambassadors watched and the man became younger as he descended and old again when he ascended the hill.

One of the most prominent roles of Coatlicue was as the goddess of corn, where she appeared in both masculine and feminine forms under the name Centeotl. Centeotl was often portrayed as a frog with numerous breasts, symbolic of the wet earth according to some commentators. Her face was painted yellow, the color of corn. During her festivals the priests wore phallic emblems in the hope of inducing Centeotl to provide Good crops for the coming year.

Another important manifestation of the goddess was as earth-goddess. She appeared with a huge, open mouth, ferocious teeth, and dressed all in white. Durán tells that when the Aztecs won a great victory under the leadership of Montezuma II, Prince Cihuacoatl, who was named after the goddess, "attired himself in the garb of the goddess Cihuacoatl. These were the female clothes which were called 'eagle garments.' "

An Aztec statue of this goddess in the Mexican Anthropological Museum portrays the cosmic aspects of the goddess as the great mother, who brings life and death. The Mexican art critic Justino Fernández said of the statue, "The whole of her vibrates and lives, inside and out, the whole of her life is life and is death; her meaning stretches in all possible directions. . . . Coatlicue is the dynamic-cosmic force giving life and maintained by death in the struggle of opposites which is so necessary that its final and most radical meaning is war. . . . Thus the dramatic beauty of Coatlicue has ultimately a warlike meaning, life and death; and this is why she is supreme, a tragic and moving beauty." (Quoted in *Mexican and Central American Mythology* (1967) by Irene Nicholson.)

A type of creator-god different from the Aztec Ometecuhtli is found among the Quiché Maya of Guatemala.

In the beginning, according to the *Popul Vuh*, the sacred book of the ancient Quiché, there was the god Hurakán hovering in the dense and primeval gloom over a watery waste. Hurakán as a mighty wind passed over the surface of the waters, saying one word, "Earth." In response to this utterance, a solid mass rose slowly from the deep.

The gods, for there were many other gods, took counsel to see what should be done next. Among the gods were Hunaphuú, Gucumatz, Xpiyacoc, and Xmucané. After some discussion it was decided to create animals, which they did. Then the gods carved wooden manikins and gave them life, but they were too puppetlike. Hurakán sent a great flood to destroy them, and all were drowned except a few handfuls whose descendants are said to be "the little monkeys that live in the woods." Later Hurakán made four perfect people.

Balam-Quitzé was the first man created by Hurakán. He was followed by Balam-Agag ("nocturnal tiger"), Mahucutan ("famous name"), and Iqui-Balam ("moon tiger"). These four were the ancestors of the Quiché, providing them with skills and knowledge.

The *Popul Vuh* tells how Balam-Quitzé provided fire for his people. One day the god Tohil appeared and Balam-

Quitzé took the god and "put him on his back" in a wooden chest he carried. As yet there was no fire, and the hero asked Tohil to provide him with it. The god gave Balam-Quitzé fire, which the culture-hero brought to his people.

After the four original men had completed their task of educating the people, they departed from the land and disappeared on Mount Hacavitz. Before the departure Balam-Quitzé left behind the Pizom-Gagal, a package which "was wrapped up and could not be unwrapped; the seam did not show because it was not seen when they wrapped it up." The mysterious package was never opened. It was called the Bundle of Greatness.

The *Popul Vuh* tells the myth of the Hunahpú and Xbalanqué, two Good hero-gods who encounter the Evil Lords of Xibalba, the lords of the underworld.

According to the *Popul Vuh*, Hun-Hunahpú, the father of Hunahpú and Xbalanqué, while playing ball with his brothers, came within the vicinity of Xibalba, the underworld in Mayan mythology. The Lords of Xibalba challenged Hun-Hunahpú to a ball game, and eventually he and his brothers were tortured and killed. Hun-Hunahpú's head was placed on a tree, which then instantly bore fruit. One day some time later Xquic ("little blood" or "blood of a woman"), the daughter of Lord Cuchumaquic, went to pick the fruit from the tree. She reached up and some spittle from the skull fell in her palm.

"In my saliva and spittle I have given you my descendants," the tree said to Xquic. The girl then gave birth to Hunahpú and Xbalanqué. As their father did before them, they encountered the Lords of Xibalba. When they arrived in the underworld, they were told to sit down.

"This is not a seat for us; it is only a hot stone," the two told the lords. They were told to enter the House of

Gloom, then the House of Knives, then the House of Jaguars, and finally the House of Bats, where they encountered the vampire-bat-god Camazotz.

To protect themselves they hid inside a blowgun. All night, bats flew around them but could not touch them. When morning came, Hunahpú went to see if it was light, and Camazotz "cut off his head." A turtle then took the place of Hunahpú's head, and the Xibalbans placed his head in the ball court. Eventually Hunahpú's head was restored.

The two heroes went on to defeat the Lords of Xibalba by using many magic means. They killed each other and then restored themselves to life. When the lords saw this wonder, they also wanted to be killed and brought back to life. The heroes obliged with the first part but did not bring the lords back to life.

The supreme god of the Incas, Viracocha ("lake of fat," or "foam of water"), though a god of creation and the generation of all life, was worshiped by having children sacrificed in his temple. The children were brought by their parents, who considered it a great honor. A child was drugged or, if very young, suckled shortly before the sacrifice, then was laid on an altar, face toward the sun—and strangled, garroted, or cut open with a knife. With their blood, *Vilacha* (or *Pipano*) was performed, which consisted of smearing the sacrificer and other celebrants with the blood. When the child had been sacrificed, a prayer was offered:

Oh, Lord, we offer thee this child, in order that thou wilt maintain us in comfort, and give us victory in war, and keep to our Lord, the Inca, his greatness and his state, and grant him wisdom that he may govern us righteously.

Viracocha made and molded the sun, endowing it with a portion of his own divinity. He placed the moon to guard and watch over the waters and winds, over the queens of the earth, and the parturition of woman. He also created Chasca, the dawn. Viracocha was invisible and incorporeal, as were his messengers, who were called *huaminca* ("the faithful soldiers") and *hayhuaypanti* ("the shining ones"). These, according to the *Relacion Anonyma de los Costumbres Antiguos de los Naturales del Piru* (1615), carried Viracocha's message to every part of the world.

The writer says that when the Indians worshiped a river, spring, mountain, or grove, "it is not that they believed that some particular divinity was there, or that it was a living thing, but because they believed that the great God, Illa Tocci [another name for Viracocha] had created and placed it there and impressed upon it some mark of distinction, beyond other objects of its class, that it might thus be designated as an appropriate spot whereat to worship the maker of all things; and this is manifest from the prayers they uttered when engaged in adoration, because they are not addressed to that mountain, or river, or cave, but to the great Illa Tocci Viracocha, who, they believed, lived in the heavens, and yet was invisibly present in that sacred object."

In prayers for the dead, Viracocha was invoked to protect the body so it would not see corruption or be lost in the earth. He conducted the soul to a haven of contentment.

South America, that vast and mysterious continent, has produced many tales of the conflict of Good and Evil. Among the Tupi Indians of Brazil, the myth of the first man and the Evil magician Valedjád captures the imagination.

At first there was no heaven or earth, only a big block of rock, smooth and beautiful. This rock was a woman, and one day it split open amid streams of blood, producing the first man, Valedjád. The rock split open a second time, producing Vab. Both Valedjád and Vab were great magicians. Since they had no wives, they took stone axes and cut down trees to create them. With the teeth of an agouti they had killed, they made a wife for each.

Valedjád was a wicked magician. Whenever he grew angry, it rained and the land was flooded. To prevent Valedjád from destroying mankind, the magician Arkoanyó hid in a tree and poured liquid wax on Valedjád as he passed by, sealing up his eyes, nostrils, and fingers so that he could no longer do Evil. To ensure that Valedjád would not free himself, a large bird flew him to the cold north country.

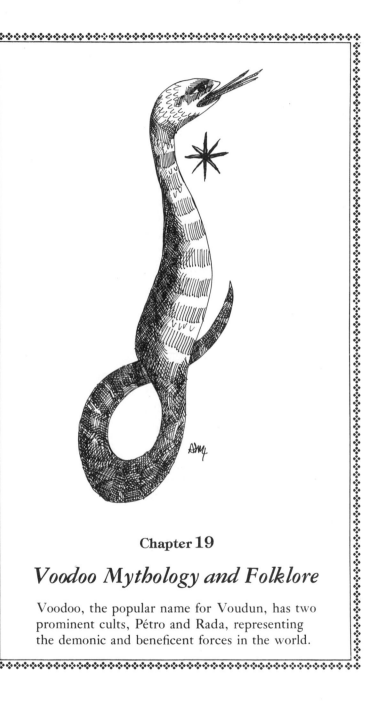

Chapter 19

Voodoo Mythology and Folklore

Voodoo, the popular name for Voudun, has two
prominent cults, Pétro and Rada, representing
the demonic and beneficent forces in the world.

According to Voodoo mythology the Hebrew Prophet Moses was taught the secrets of the Voodoo cult by Jethro, the shepherd-priest of the Midianite tribe called the Kenites. Fleeing from Egypt after slaying an Egyptian, Moses tended Jethro's sheep near Mount Horeb, where he experienced his great Theophany when Yahweh-God manifested himself in the Burning Bush (Exodus 3). Moses married Jethro's shepherdess daughter, Zipporah, who bore him two sons (Exodus 18:1–4). The Voodoo accounts add that the children were mulatto. This so upset Aaron and Miriam, the brother and sister of Moses, that Moses eventually divorced Zipporah. The Voodoo Loas, ancestor spirits or gods, were so angry at Moses's action that they caused his sister Miriam to turn white with leprosy.

In the Biblical account both Aaron and Miriam criticized Moses for his marriage to Zipporah, an Ethiopian, but actually both were jealous of Moses's leadership position. Miriam was afflicted with a leprous condition and was cured after Moses's intercession with Yahweh.

The Voodoo reworking of the Biblical legend is an excellent example of how this living religion combines both Christian and African beliefs. Such a combination, however, has upset many scholars. The august scholarly work in thirteen volumes *Encyclopedia of Religion and Ethics* (1918), by James Hastings, ends its entry on Voodoo with a warning that "few white people realize the menace of voodoo due to its absolute power over a certain class of minds." One may excuse this remark as being dated, but the current *Dictionary of Comparative Religion* (1970), by S.G.F. Brandon, characterizes Voodoo as a "form of devil worship" in which the priests of the cult must "undergo horrible and disgusting tests." If both scholars had looked at Voodoo without color prejudice, they would have discovered that far from being limited to certain kinds of minds or incorporating any particularly horrible rites, it contains elements found in all major mythologies.

Voodoo's basic belief is that man's material body is animated by a soul, spirit, psyche, or self which is called *gros-bon-ange*. This nonmaterial self does not die when the body dies but lives on and can achieve the status of a Loa, or god. The Loas can be called down by a Houn'gan or Mam'bo (priest or priestess). When the Loas descend, they enter *govis*, jars placed upon the Voodoo altar, or by possession they "mount" a worshiper. A Loa that takes complete possession of a person controls all the actions of that person, while the possessed loses all consciousness of self. The possessed person, the *cheval* (the French word for horse, the person being "mounted" by the Loa), may prophesy, dance, and perform magic and other actions which are not recalled when the possessed awakens.

A young girl, for example, who is mounted by an old Loa will become as feeble and practically as speechless as the Loa was in life. Yet if an old man is mounted by a vigorous young Loa, he will act as a young man. Generally the entire personality of the mounted person is erased during this *crise de Loa*. Normally unable to walk, the sick dance and leap about during the Loa-crisis.

The Voodoo rituals in Haiti are conducted in the Oum'phor, a temple resembling Moses's design for the Ark of the Covenant and Tabernacles described in Exodus (25–27). The Oum'phor consists of a large area, usually covered, with a center post, the Poteau-mitan, which recalls the staff of Moses. All important rites are conducted around the Poteau-mitan, the top of which is believed to be the center of the sky, and the bottom the center of hell. The Poteau-mitan is usually square and set in a circular masonry pedestal, the *socle*. Around the pedestal are triangular niches. The *socle* itself is a form of altar (called *pe*) on which are placed various ritualistic implements. These include *pots-de-tete*, jars containing spirits of the people who worship at the Oum'phor, and *govis*, jars which receive the Loas when they are called down by the Houn'gan or Mam'bo.

The rites conducted at the Oum'phor are generally of two types: Pétro and Rada. The Pétro rite is believed to have been derived from a powerful Voodoo priest who was one of the first settlers of Haiti. Although Pétro is usually associated with violence, especially in the popular imagination, it can be viewed as representing the more aggressive aspects of nature.

The other rite, Rada, represents the protective guardian powers of the cosmos. Both rites often invoke the same Loas: the ancestral spirits, or gods.

Among the most important Loas are Danbhalah Houe-Do, the serpent god, the oldest of the Loas; Erzulie, goddess who represents both Good and Evil; Ghede, god of the Dead; Legba, the Christ-figure mentioned earlier; and Manman Brigitte, who is invoked by people constantly embroiled in disputes.

Danbhalah Houe-Do's symbol is a snake arched in the path of the sun as it travels across the sky. Sometimes half the arch is made up of his female counterpart, Ayida (or Aida Wedo), the rainbow, who in some beliefs is merely another form of the goddess Erzulie. When Danbhalah Houe-Do comes down and mounts a worshiper, the person loses the power to speak and can only hiss. Danbhalah Houe-Do is often invoked in the Pétro rite, but Erzulie is invoked in both Pétro and Rada rites.

Erzulie combines the qualities of the great mother-goddess found in ancient Near Eastern mythologies; she is both beneficent and demonic. In her demonic aspect she represents jealousy, vengeance, and discord, causing people she mounts to twist in fantastic convulsions and even practice cannibalism. In her beneficent role she is love, perpetual help, good will, health, beauty, and fortune. Erzulie's symbol is a heart pierced by swords, which is also one of the main symbols of the Virgin Mary in Christianity. Sometimes statues of the Virgin are used in Voodoo ceremonies to represent the goddess Erzulie.

The combination of beneficent and demonic forces found in Erzulie is also found in Ghede, who is god of the Dead and Lord of Life. In the chamber dedicated to his worship, a sculptured phallus lies next to a gravedigger's tools, symbolizing that Ghede is both the beginning and the end of all things. His symbol is the cross. Also connected with the dead are Baron Samedi, Mait Carrefour, and Grand Bois d'Ilet. Baron Samedi is Lord of the Cemeteries and a god of the crossroads, somewhat resembling Legba. Mait Carrefour is master of the demons of the night and is invoked for protection against them. Grand Bois d'Ilet is Lord of the Night and Night Forests.

One of the most popular figures among the Loas, Manman Brigitte, does not have her own altar at the Voodoo Oum'phor but is worshiped in the main cemetery of Port-au-Prince, Haiti. Her sacred elm tree was cut down by the government and Roman Catholic Church authorities because too many people were seen praying to Manman Brigitte by placing lighted candles at the foot of her tree. On August 15, 1975, *The New York Times* reported that "hundreds of pilgrims travel each year to a crumbling tomb in St. Louis Cemetery to rub their feet three times in gravel and scrawl a red 'X' in tribute to the leader they believe lies there—Marie Laveau, the voodoo queen." Marie Laveau made her reputation in the 1830s "telling fortunes and casting spells."

The dead and cemeteries naturally bring to mind the most well-known aspect of Voodoo belief, the zombie, a term for a soulless body brought back to "life" in a cataleptic state of automation. The term derives from the West

African python-god Danhgbi, who entered the body of his priests and spoke through their mouths in a strange and "unnatural voice." Worship of the python-god was brought to the New World, and in New Orleans there were ministers to the serpent-god, a king and queen (or papa and mama) who communicated the will of the sacred serpent to his followers. They held office for life, and to disobey them was an offense against the god. In New Orleans, "voodooism" (according to *The Picayune's Guide to New Orleans,* 1896) "was, in fact, a system of fetish idolatry. Its main features consisted of the worship of the serpent, and *Li Grand Zombi* was the mysterious power which guarded and overshadowed the faithful 'voudou' and was held sacred. The serpent was kept by the priestess or queen of the voodoos in an exquisitely carved box on a table in her own bedchamber. Candles were kept continually burning around it and two voodoos were specially delegated to watch these lights day and night."

In Haiti a zombie is one of the most dreaded of beings, and its existence is not doubted. The Criminal Code of Haiti says, "Also shall be qualified as attempted murder the employment which may be made against any person of substances, which, without causing actual death, produce a lethargic coma more or less prolonged. If, after the administering of such substances, the person has been buried, the act shall be considered murder no matter what result follows."

To avoid creation of zombies, the Haitians take measures to make sure that a body is truly lifeless. Sometimes a knife is plunged through the heart, other times plants may be placed in the coffin containing so many seeds that anyone coming to take the body, being forced to count them, would be caught by daybreak.

Zombies are found not only in Haiti but also in movies. Victor Halperin's *White Zombie* (1932) was the first sound film of many on the subject. The term *zombie* was also applied to a strong rum drink, said to leave the drinker apparently lifeless with intoxication. In a Ritz Brothers film, the three comedians walk up to a bartender and order "three zombies."

"I can see that," the bartender replies, "but what'll you have to drink?"

Epilogue

WE HAVE EXPLORED the problem of Good and Evil from ancient Egypt to present-day Voodoo in the hope of shedding some light on the matter through mythology and folklore. Since the Prologue opened with a fable of Tolstoy, it also seems fitting to end with a tale, *The Devil and the Lord*, a folktale from the American West.

One hot day Jesus and the Devil were walking side by side across the hot sands. The two were arguing.

"Satan," said Jesus, "why are you so Evil? Why don't you try to do Good sometimes?"

"My Lord," replied the Devil, "you ask too much of me. I can't be Good. I've been Evil for too long. Even if I did a Good deed, it would still be branded as Evil."

"What foolish talk," said Jesus.

"No," replied the Devil. "I speak the truth. Let me prove it to you. Do you see the muddy lake near those trees yonder?"

"Yes."

"And do you see that cow which is wading into the lake for a drink of water?"

"Yes," replied Jesus.

"Very well, then," said the Devil. "Now with your power let me see you cause that cow to be bogged in that mud."

Jesus raised his hand and called upon God. Immediately the cow sank to her belly in the soft mud and began to struggle.

"Now," said the Devil, "let's hide behind the prickly pear to see what will happen."

The two hid and soon a cowboy came riding by the lake and spotted the cow in the mud.

"Ah," said the cowboy, "the Devil must be at work causing this poor cow to get stuck in the mud. I'll call some of my friends to help get her out."

"You see," said the Devil to Jesus, "how I get the blame. Now watch, I'll get the cow out and see what happens."

As soon as the cowboy was out of sight the Devil came from behind the tree, flopped his tail, rattled his teeth, and blinked his eyes. Immediately the cow was raised from the lake and was safe.

Not long afterward the cowboy returned with some help to save the cow and discovered she was safe.

"The good Lord must have saved the cow," said the cowboy in relief.

"See," whispered the Devil to Jesus, "even if I do a good deed, the credit is given to you, while all the Evil deeds are credited to me. I am punished for all the Evil of men, while you are rewarded for all the virtues of men. Is that justice? What would it avail me if I should be Good?"

Annotated Bibliography

I HAVE NOT burdened the reader with footnotes but have instead compiled an annotated bibliography, chapter by chapter. Though the bibliography does contain the major works and sources used in writing the book, it makes no pretense at completeness.

Many works cited are available in different editions, especially the earlier books on mythology and folklore. When a book has been reprinted and I have used the reprint edition, I have indicated the earlier publication information. Where the information is incomplete, it is because the reprint has not given the information.

For ease of reference I have arranged the bibliography according to titles.

General Reference Works on Mythology, Folklore, and Religion

Adonis, Attis, Osiris: Studies in the History of Oriental Religion, by James George Frazer; University Books, New Hyde Park, New York, 1961.
  Part IV of *The Golden Bough*, printed as one volume. Index.

Bray's University Dictionary of Mythology, by Frank Chapin Bray; Thomas Y. Crowell Co., New York, 1964.
  A dictionary of mythology, with little folklore, divided into sections, such as Greek mythology A to Z, etc. Often, however, the information is inaccurate. Index.

Bulfinch's Mythology, by Thomas Bulfinch; Thomas Y. Crowell, New York, 1970.
  An edition containing *The Age of Fable* (1855), *The Age of Chivalry* (1858), and *Legends of Charlemagne* (1863). Popular, nineteenth-century approach, leaving out the "distasteful" elements in myths. Helpful Dictionary and Index.

Dictionary of All Scriptures and Myths, by G. A. Gaskell; The Julian Press, Inc., New York, 1960.

Muddled, misleading work with strong occult bias, but valuable for its numerous quotations.

Dictionary of Comparative Religion, edited by S. G. F. Brandon; Charles Scribner's Sons, New York, 1970.

Unbalanced work, difficult to use, with often anti-Christian bias, though entries on Buddhist and Hindu myths and religion are often good. Synoptic index. General index.

Dictionary of Mythology, Folklore and Symbols, by Gertrude Jobes; The Scarecrow Press, Inc., New York, 1962.

A three-volume work, often unreliable in its entries, particularly on interpretations which tend to be of the nineteenth-century Solar School of Max Müller. Valuable for the variant spellings of many names and for its index.

A Dictionary of Non-Christian Religions, by Geoffrey Parrinder; The Westminster Press, Philadelphia, 1971.

A good, one-volume guide for religion and sacred books.

Encyclopedia of Religion and Ethics, edited by James Hastings; Charles Scribner's Sons, New York.

A thirteen-volume work, dated and prejudiced in many articles, but filled with information. One-volume index.

An Encyclopedia of Religions, by Maurice A Canney; G. Routledge & Sons, Ltd., London, 1921. Reissued by Gale Research Company, Detroit, 1970.

A one-volume work, dated in many respects, and mainly concerned with Christianity. No index.

Encyclopedia of Superstitions, by E. and M. A. Radford; Hutchinson of London, 1948.

Excellent one-volume work, dealing mainly with English folklore.

Everyman's Dictionary of Non-Classical Mythology, edited by Egerton Sykes; J.M. Dent & Sons, London, 1952.

A short, one-volume work that leaves much information out, but serves as a quick reference. Often information is misleading or incomplete, however. The cross-referencing is often of little help to the reader.

The Great Mother of the Gods, by Grant Showerman; 1901. Reissued by Argonaut, Inc., Chicago, 1969.

A short study covering various aspects of the mother-goddess. Index.

The History of the Devil and the Idea of Evil, by Paul Carus; Open Court Publishing, 1900. Reissued by Land's End Press, New York, 1969.

A popular, fully illustrated study of the subject, containing excellent sources. No bibliography. Index.

Mythologies of All Races, edited by Louis Herbert Gray; Marshall Jones Company, 1916. Reissued by Cooper Square Publishers, Inc., New York, 1964.

A thirteen-volume work dealing with Greek, Roman, Eddic, Celtic, Slavic, Finno-Ugric, Siberian, Semitic, Indian, Iranian, Armenian, African, Chinese, Japanese, Oceanic, North American, Latin American, Egyptian, and Far Eastern mythologies. Usefulness varies from volume to volume, depending on the author. A one-volume index.

The New Golden Bough, edited by Theodor H. Gaster; Criterion Books, New York, 1959.

A new abridgment of the classic work of James George Frazer. Additional notes, etc. Index.

New Larousse Encyclopedia of Mythology; Prometheus Press, New York, 1959.

A one-volume, heavily illustrated work by various hands which varies in content and usefulness. Short bibliography. Index.

The New Schaff-Herzog Encyclopedia of Religious Knowledge, edited by Samuel Macauley Jackson; 1907. Reissued by Baker Book House, Grand Rapids, 1949.

A thirteen-volume work from the German, covering mainly Christian themes. One-volume index. Bibliographical appendix.

The Religion of the Primitives, by Alexander LeRoy; The Macmillan Co., New York, 1922.

A general study by a Christian missionary. Index.

Religion in Primitive Society, by Edward Norbeck; Harper & Row, New York, 1961.

General study of the subject. Bibliography. Index.

Religions of the World, edited by Geoffrey Parrinder; Grosset & Dunlap, New York, 1971.

General study written by various hands. Bibliography. Index.

Standard Dictionary of Folklore, Mythology and Legend, edited by Maria Leach; Funk & Wagnalls, New York, 1972.

An extensive work, written by many "experts" in the field. Wide coverage of folklore, but lacking in mythology and religion.

Twentieth Century Encyclopedia of Religious Knowledge, edited by Lefferts A. Loetscher; Baker Book House, Grand Rapids, 1955.

A two-volume extension of *The New Schaff-Herzog Encyclopedia of Religious Knowledge* covering mainly Christian themes.

Bible Translations, Dictionaries, Commentaries, and Handbooks

The Cambridge History of the Bible, edited by P.R. Ackroyd and C.F. Evans; Cambridge University Press, New York, 1970.

A three-volume work covering all aspects of the Bible. Indexes.

A Dictionary of the Bible, edited by James Hastings; Charles Scribner's Sons, New York, 1898.

A four-volume work dealing with every aspect of the Bible. An additional volume was included in 1904, bringing it up to that date.

Dictionary of the Bible, edited by James Hastings; Charles Scribner's Sons, New York, 1963.

A one-volume dictionary, revised by Frederick C. Grant and H.H. Rowley, from Hastings's five-volume dictionary.

Dictionary of the Bible, by John L. McKenzie; The Bruce Publishing Co., Milwaukee, 1965.

A one-volume Catholic dictionary.

Encyclopedic Dictionary of the Bible, edited by Louis F. Hartman; McGraw-Hill Book Co., Inc., New York, 1963.

A good one-volume dictionary from the Dutch *Bijbels Woordenboek* (1954–1957).

Good News Bible; American Bible Society, New York, 1976.

A modern, simple version of the Bible with notes, maps, and other aids.

The Holy Bible, translated by Ronald Knox; Burns and Oates, London, 1955.

A translation from the Latin Vulgate in the light of the Hebrew and Greek originals.

The Holy Bible, Confraternity Version; Benziger Brothers, Inc., New York, 1950.

A translation made up of the Old Douay Version of the seventeenth century and a modern version of some books.

The Interpreter's Bible; Abingdon Press, New York/Nashville, 1952.

A twelve-volume work with the King James Version and Revised Standard Version as texts. Numerous general articles. Indexes.

The Jerome Biblical Commentary, edited by R.E. Brown, J.A. Fitzmyer, and R.E. Murphy; Prentice-Hall, Inc., Englewood Cliffs, New Jersey, 1968.

A good one-volume Catholic commentary. Index.

The Jerusalem Bible, edited by Alexander Jones; Doubleday & Co., Inc., Garden City, 1966.

Vigorous modern translation by Catholics with doctrinal notes which must be used with caution.

The Oxford Annotated Bible with the Apocrypha Revised Standard Version, edited by H.G. May and B.M. Metzger; Oxford University Press, New York, 1965.

A handy one-volume annotated RSV Bible with charts, tables, indexes.

Peake's Commentary on the Bible, edited by M. Black and H.H. Rowley; Thomas Nelson and Sons, Ltd., London, 1962.

A good one-volume commentary on the Bible. Index.

Chapter 1: Egyptian Mythology

Ancient Egyptian Religion, by Henri Frankfort; Columbia University Press, New York, 1948. Reissued by Harper Torchbooks, New York, 1961.

A short survey of the gods, state, way of life, art, and literature. Index.

The Ancient Egyptians: A Sourcebook of Their Writings, edited by Adolf Erman; translated by Aylward M. Blackman; Harper Torchbooks, New York, 1966.

This book was originally published in German in 1923 and translated into English in 1927 as *The Literature of the Ancient Egyptians*. An interesting anthology, though many of the translations are stiff and awkward.

The Book of the Dead: The Hieroglyphic Transcript of the Papyrus of Ani, translated by E.A. Wallis Budge; various editions, 1890, 1894, 1913. Reissued by University Books, New Hyde Park, New York, 1960, from 1913 Medici Society edition plus a 1920 British Museum pamphlet on The Book of the Dead prepared by Budge.

A major source book but difficult to read. Budge often contradicts what he wrote in *The Gods of the Egyptians* (1904). In addition transliteration of Egyptian names varies in both books, making it difficult for the reader to sort out the gods.

Egyptian Literature, edited by Epiphanius Wilson; revised edition, The Colonial Press, London and New York, 1901.

Comprising Egyptian tales, hymns, litanies, invocations, The Book of the Dead, and cuneiform writings. A good selection of the literature, containing the best that was known in the nineteenth century. The merits of the translations vary in each work.

Egyptian Religion: Egyptian Ideas of the Future Life, by E.A. Wallis Budge; London, 1900. Reissued by Bell Publishing Company, New York, 1969.

A short study dealing with the cult of Osiris. No index.

The Genesis of British Egyptology: 1549–1906, by John David Wortham; University of Oklahoma Press, 1971.

A chronological account of the origins and early development of British Egyptology. Notes. Bibliography. Index.

The Gods of the Egyptians, or Studies in Egyptian Mythology, by E.A. Wallis Budge; The Open Court Publishing Co., Chicago, and Methuen & Company, London, 1904. Reprinted by Dover Publications, New York, 1969.

The classic study of Egypt's gods by the one-time Keeper of the Egyptian and Assyrian Antiquities in the British Museum. The book is filled with information, texts, and translations but is very poorly arranged and often contradicts itself from one section to another. Budge's transliteration of Egyptian names differs in many cases from the system used in his edition of *The Book of the Dead* (1890, 1894, 1913).

Life in Ancient Egypt and Assyria, by Gaston C.C. Maspero; Frederick Ungar Publishing Co., New York, 1971. Republication of the 1892 English edition of *Lectures historiques: Histoire ancienne: Egypte, Assyrie*.

A short overview of life in ancient Egypt, written in a narrative style attempting to recreate the era. Some chapters are successful, others forced.

The Literature of Ancient Egypt: An Anthology of Stories, Instructions and Poetry, edited by William Kelly Simpson; Yale University Press, New Haven and London, 1972.

An excellent anthology of numerous texts, many relating to legendary and mythological subjects. The translations vary in merit.

Living Architecture: Egyptian, by Jean-Louis de Cenival; Grosset & Dunlap, New York, 1964. Preface by Marcel Breuer.

A brilliant study of Egyptian architecture with excellent photographs and plans of the various structures and art works.

Love Songs of the New Kingdom, edited and translated by John L. Foster; Charles Scribner's Sons, New York, 1974.

A facet of the Egyptians often overlooked, in lovely verse translations. Introduction and index.

The Mummy, by E.A. Wallis Budge; second edition, 1894. Reissued by Causeway Books, New York, 1974.

A classic study of mummification. Index.

Mythologies of the World, chapter on "Mythology in Ancient Egypt," by Rudolf Anthes, edited by Samuel Noah Kramer; Doubleday Anchor Original, 1961.

A long essay on the subject, somewhat heavy-handed but containing interesting remarks on the Eye of Ra.

Osiris: The Egyptian Religion of Resurrection, by E.A. Wallis Budge; Philip Lee Warner, 1911. New edition University Books, New Hyde Park, New York, 1961.

A lengthy, elaborate study of Osiris and his place in Egyptian mythology, with emphasis on Osiris's African origin. In transliteration of Egyptian names, Budge varies with some of his other books, making referencing difficult. Index.

Popular Stories of Ancient Egypt, by Gaston C.C. Maspero; translated by A.S. Johns; University Books, New Hyde Park, New York, 1967. An

English edition of *Les contes populaires de l'Egypte ancienne*, 1882, translated 1915.

The volume contains seventeen complete stories and six fragments, many with a folkloric base.

Wings of the Falcon: Life and Thought in Ancient Egypt, translated and edited by Joseph Kaster; Holt, Rinehart and Winston, New York, 1968.

A lively introduction to Egypt with a fair amount on its gods and mythological literature.

Chapter 2: Babylonian and Assyrian Mythologies

The Ancient Near East: An Anthology of Texts and Pictures, edited by James B. Pritchard; Princeton University Press, Princeton, New Jersey, 1958.

A collection of important texts with illustrations and notes. Index and glossary.

Ancient Near Eastern Texts Relating to the Old Testament, edited by James B. Pritchard; Princeton University Press, Princeton, New Jersey, 1955.

An important collection, fully annotated. Index of Biblical names.

Babylonian and Assyrian Literature, edited by Epiphanius Wilson; The Colonial Press, New York, 1901.

A collection of various texts of great interest. The translations tend to be rather awkward.

The Epic of Gilgamesh, translated by N.K. Sandars; Penguin Books, Baltimore, 1960.

A prose version of the epic with a long introduction and glossary of names.

Gilgamesh: A Verse Narrative, by Herbert Mason; Houghton Mifflin Company, Boston, 1971.

A modern poetic retelling of the epic of Gilgamesh based on a scholarly translation.

Myths & Legends of Babylonia and Assyria, by Lewis Spence; George G. Harrap & Co., London, 1916. Reissued by Gale Research Company, Detroit, 1975.

A popular study but often confusing in its retellings of the myths. Glossary and index.

Near Eastern Mythology: Mesopotamia, Syria, Palestine, by John Gray; Hamlyn Publishing Group, Ltd., London, 1969.
   A short, illustrated study of the subject. Often quite good. Reading list and index.

Poems of Heaven and Hell from Ancient Mesopotamia, translated by N.K. Sandars; Penguin Books, Baltimore.
   An excellent translation and collection with notes and glossary of names.

The Religion of Babylonia and Assyria, by Morris Jastrow; Ginn & Company, Publishers, Boston, 1898.
   Massive study of the subject. Bibliography and index.

The Religion of Babylonia and Assyria, by Theophilus G. Pinches; Archibald Constable and Co., London, 1906.
   A short, concise guide. No index.

Ugarit and Minoan Crete, by Cyrus H. Gordon; W.W. Norton & Co., Inc., New York, 1966.
   A book containing texts in translation as well as a study of the subject. Index.

Chapter 3: Persian Mythology and Zoroastrianism

The Gulistan or Rose Garden of Sadi, translated by Edward Rehatsek, 1888. Reissued by G.P. Putnam's Sons, New York, 1965.
   An edition of the 1888 translation with a new introduction by G.M. Wickens.

The Masnavi of Rumi, translated by E.H. Whinfield. Reissued by E.P. Dutton & Co., Inc., New York, 1975.
   A reissue of a turn-of-the-century abridged translation of the work.

Persian Folktales, translated by Alfred Kurti; G. Bell & Sons, London, 1971.
   Originally published as *Persische Volksmärchen* (1958), this translation from the German contains a good choice of tales as well as notes on sources.

Persian Literature, edited by Richard J.H. Gottheil; The Colonial Press, New York, 1900.
   An anthology containing *The Shah-Nameh*, abridged in prose and verse; *The Rubaiyat; The Divan;* and *The Gulistan.*

Persian Mythology, by John R. Hinnells; Hamlyn Publishing Group, Ltd., London, 1973.

Excellent, illustrated short study. Bibliography and index.

Persian Poems: An Anthology of Verse Translations, edited by A.J. Arberry; J.M. Dent & Sons, Ltd., London, 1954.

Good selection, with index of poets, short biographies, index of translators, and short glossary.

The Persian Poets, edited by Nathan Haskell Doles and B.M. Walker; Thomas Y. Crowell & Co., New York, 1901.

Good selection with introduction.

The Shah-Namah of Fardusi, translated by Alexander Rogers, 1907. Reissued by Heritage Publishers, Delhi, 1973.

An abridged translation of the epic poem in prose and verse.

Chapter 4: Hebrew Mythology and Jewish Folklore

Ancient Judaism, by Max Weber; The Free Press, Glencoe, Illinois, 1952.

A sociological study of Judaism. Notes, glossary, and index.

Aspects of Rabbinic Theology, by Solomon Schechter; The Macmillan Company, 1909. Reissued by Schocken Books, Inc., New York, 1961.

An excellent introduction to Rabbinic thought with chapters on the Yezer Hara. Good index.

The Book of the Letters: A Mystical Alef-Bait, by Lawrence Kushner; Harper & Row, Publishers, New York, 1975.

A mystical treatment of the Hebrew alphabet with numerous tales and explanations from folklore.

Customs and Folkways of Jewish Life, by Theodor H. Gaster; William Sloane Associates Publishers, New York, 1955.

A reissue of *The Holy and the Profane*, covering various aspects of Jewish folk beliefs and rituals. Source references and bibliography. Index.

The Post-Biblical History of the Jews, by Werner Keller, and Richard and Clara Winston; Harcourt, Brace & World, Inc., New York, 1966.

Well-written study with an additional chapter by Ronald Sanders, "A History of the Jews in America." Bibliography and index.

The Encyclopedia of the Jewish Religion, edited by R.J. Swi Werblowsky and Geoffrey Wigoder; Holt, Rinehart and Winston, Inc., New York, 1965.

A concise and helpful book on various aspects of Judaism.

Folktales of Israel, edited and translated by Dov Noy and Gene Baharav; The University of Chicago Press, Chicago, 1963.

Part of the series *Folktales of the World*, under the editorship of Richard M. Dorson. Excellent collection with scholarly notes. Glossary. Bibliography. Index of Motifs and Index of Tale Types, etc., plus general index.

The Great Jewish Books and Their Influence on History, edited by Samuel Caplan and Harold U. Ribalow; Horizon Press, 1953. Reissued by Washington Square Press, New York, 1963.

A short anthology, with introductions. Selected bibliography.

The Guide for the Perplexed, by Moses Maimonides, translated by M. Friedlander; Routledge & Kegan Publishing, Ltd., London, 1904.

A classic Jewish work having profound influence on Jewish and Christian thought; with an introduction and Index of Scriptural Passages.

Hebrew Literature, edited by Epiphanius Wilson; The Colonial Press, London, New York, 1901.

A selection of Hebrew literature comprising excerpts from the *Talmud*, the *Lesser Holy Assembly* from the *Kabalah*, and a selection of Hebrew poems. No index.

The Hebrew Scriptures: An Introduction to Their Literature and Religious Ideas, by Samuel Sandmel; Alfred A. Knopf, New York, 1963.

Jewish study of the Old Testament. Selected annotated bibliography and subject index.

Invitation to the Talmud, by Jacob Neusner; Harper & Row, Publishers, New York, 1973.

A short introduction to a vast, often complex subject. Biographical supplement. Index.

The Mishnah, edited and translated by Herbert Danby; Oxford University Press, London, 1933.

Often the notes are too brief to be of much help to the reader.

Philo with an English Translation, edited and translated by F.H. Colson and G.H. Whitaker; Harvard University Press, Cambridge, Mass., 1929.

A ten-volume translation with notes of the major Jewish allegorical interpretation of the Hebrew Bible. Indexes.

A Treasury of Jewish Folklore, edited by Nathan Ausubel; Crown Publishers, New York, 1948.

An excellent anthology, covering stories, traditions, legends, humor, wisdom, and folk song. Glossary and index.

A Treasury of Jewish Poetry, edited by Nathan and Maryann Ausubel; Crown Publishers, Inc., New York, 1957.

A collection of Jewish poets with a long, good introduction. Major drawback is that the book is not arranged chronologically, but divided into subject areas, such as "The Spirit of Man," "Messiah and Redemption," etc. Index of titles. Biographical index of authors.

A Treasury of Yiddish Poetry, edited by Irving Howe and Eliezer Greenberg; Holt, Rinehart and Winston, New York, 1969.

Interesting anthology with long, good introduction. Glossary and index of poets and titles.

What You Should Know About Jewish Religion, History, Ethics and Culture, by Rabbi Sidney L. Markowitz; The Citadel Press, New York, 1955.

A short introduction to contemporary Judaism, covering such topics as the *Talmud*, religion, holidays, and fast days. Bibliography and index.

Chapter 5: Christian Mythology and Folklore

Apocryphal Gospels, Acts and Revelations, edited and translated by Alexander Walker; T. & T. Clark, Edinburgh, 1890.

An excellent selection of the tales and legends not included in the New Testament. Index.

The Apocryphal New Testament, edited and translated by Montague Rhodes James; Oxford University Press, 1924.

An excellent selection but a stiff translation of the various apocryphal gospels, acts, epistles, and apocalypses not included in the New Testament. Index of subjects.

A Biographical Dictionary of the Saints, by F.G. Holweck; B. Herder Book Company, St. Louis, 1924.

Short entries on numerous saints.

The Book of Concord, edited and translated by Theodore G. Tappert; Fortress Press, Philadelphia, 1959.

A collection of the Confessions of the Evangelical Lutheran Church. Index.

The Book of Saints; The Macmillan Co., New York, 1947.

A dictionary of saints extracted from the Roman and other martyrologies. The fourth edition with a Calendar of Saints.

A Catholic Dictionary, edited by Donald Attwater; The Macmillan Co., New York, 1958.

A one-volume dictionary covering general Catholic subjects.

Concise Dictionary of Proper Names and Notable Matters in the Works of Dante, by Paget Toynbee, 1914. Reissued by Phaeton Press, New York, 1968.

Though written in English, the listings in the dictionary are under the Italian names. The book is of help on many matters.

A Dictionary of Saints, by Donald Attwater; P.J. Kenedy & Sons, New York.

An A to Z listing of saints which also serves as an index to Attwater's revised edition of Alban Butler's *Lives of the Saints.*

Dante Alighieri: The Divine Comedy, translated by Lawrence Grant White; Pantheon Books, New York, 1948.

A blank verse translation, no notes, with illustrations by Doré.

Dante: The Divine Comedy, translated by Louis Biancolli; Washington Square Press, New York, 1966.

Italian text faced with a blank verse translation on the other side of page. No notes.

La Divina Commedia di Dante Alighieri, edited by C.H. Grandgent; D.C. Heath and Co., Boston, 1933.

The Italian text with notes in English. Index.

The Divine Comedy, by Dante Alighieri, translated by G.L. Bickersteth; Harvard University Press, Cambridge, 1965.

Dual texts, Italian and English, in the meter of the original, with introduction.

The Divine Comedy, by Dante Alighieri, translated by Henry F. Cary; Crown Publishing, New York.

An edition of one of the most reprinted translations into blank verse. Notes.

The Divine Comedy of Dante Alighieri, translated by Charles Eliot Norton; Houghton Mifflin Company, Boston, 1920.

    A prose translation issued in 1891, 1892, and 1902, in three parts, now bound as one volume.

The Early Christian Fathers, edited and translated by Henry Bettenson; Oxford University Press, London, 1956.

    A selection from the writings of the fathers of the church from Saint Clement of Rome to Saint Athanasius. Index.

Early English Christian Poetry, edited and translated by Charles W. Kennedy; Oxford University Press, 1952.

    A collection of poems translated in alliterative verse with a critical commentary. Index.

English Religious Drama of the Middle Ages, by Hardin Craig; Oxford University Press, London, 1955.

    An extensive study. Bibliography and index.

The Essential Augustine, edited by Vernon J. Bourke; Mentor-Omega, New American Libarary, 1964.

    A good selection of the saint's writings. Appendices and index.

The Lives of the Saints, by Alban Butler; P.J. Kenedy & Sons, New York.

    A four-volume, revised edition by Herbert Thurston and Donald Attwater. Often dull, but filled with information.

The Lore of the New Testament, edited by Joseph Gaer; Little, Brown and Company, Boston, 1952.

    A collection of legends and tales written around New Testament incidents, with notes and list of sources. Excellent reading list with notes.

Selected Writings of Martin Luther, edited by Theodore G. Tappert; Fortress Press, Philadelphia, 1967.

    Four-volume anthology containing major works of Luther. Index in each volume.

The Middle English Miracles of the Virgin, edited by Beverly Boyd; The Huntington Library, San Marino, Calif. 1964.

    A collection of Middle English poems on the Virgin, with notes, index.

John Milton: Complete Poems and Major Prose, edited by Merritt Y. Hughes; The Odyssey Press, New York, 1957.
A fully annotated edition of the poems with the reference to mythology. Index of names.

Milton: A Critical Heritage, edited by John T. Shawcross; Barnes & Noble, Inc., New York, 1970.
A varied collection of critical remarks up to the eighteenth century on Milton's works. Select index.

A Milton Dictionary, by Edward S. LeComte; Philosophical Library, New York, 1961.
A short dictionary of Milton's works. Of value for quick reference.

The Romantics on Milton: Formal Essays and Critical Asides, edited by Joseph Anthony Wittreich, Jr.; The Press of Case Western Reserve University, Cleveland, 1970.
A varied collection from William Blake to John Keats on Milton's works. Index.

Myth and Guilt: The Crime and Punishment of Mankind, by Theodor Reik; George Braziller, Inc., New York, 1957.
A study of guilt in Western society with emphasis on the Christian and Jewish interpretations. No index.

New Catholic Encyclopedia; McGraw-Hill Book Co., New York, 1967.
A modern, fifteen-volume work covering not only Catholic topics.

Old English Poetry, edited and translated by J. Duncan Spaeth; Princeton University Press, New Jersey, 1921.
Translations into alliterative verse with introductions and notes.

The Other Jesus, edited by Robert O. Ballou; Doubleday & Company, Garden City, New York, 1972.
A narrative based on the apocryphal stories of Jesus not included in the Bible but part of Christian tradition. Contains an identification of sources.

Paradise Lost, by John Milton, 1667. Reissued by The Scholar Press Ltd., Menston, England, 1968.
A facsimile of the 1667 edition of *Paradise Lost*.

Paul of Tarsus, by Joseph Holzner; B. Herder Book Co., St. Louis, 1945.
A Catholic view of Paul's life and work. Index.

Religion and Society in the Age of Saint Augustine, by Peter Brown; Harper & Row, Publishers, New York, 1972.

A study of the saint and his times. Index.

Basic Writings of Saint Augustine, edited by Whitney J. Oates; Random House, New York, 1948.

A two-volume selection of the writings of the saint, including the main works. Indexes.

Basic Writings of Saint Thomas Aquinas, by Anton C. Pegis; Random House, New York, 1945.

A two-volume selection of the writings of the saint.

Select Translations from Old English Prose, edited by Albert S. Cook and Chauncey B. Tinker; Harvard University Press, Cambridge, Mass., 1908.

Work contains the Medieval "Harrowing of Hell." Index.

The Sources of the Doctrines of the Fall and Original Sin, by F.R. Tennant; 1903. Reissued by Schocken Books, New York, 1968.

A classic study with a new introduction by Mary Frances Thelen. Index of subjects.

Theological Dictionary, by Karl Rahner and Herbert Vorgrimler; Herder and Herder, New York, 1965.

A Roman Catholic one-volume dictionary translated from the German by Richard Strachan.

Chapter 6: Armenian Mythology and Folklore

Armenian Literature, edited by Robert Arnot; The Colonial Press, New York, 1901.

An anthology containing poetry, drama, and folklore.

Armenian Mythology, Mardiros H. Ananikian; Marshall Jones Company, 1925. Reissued by Cooper Square Publishers, Inc., New York, 1964.

Volume VII of *The Mythology of All Races*. Concise study with notes, bibliography. No index, except in final volume of full set.

Chapter 7: Islamic Mythology and Folklore

Anthology of Islamic Literature from the Rise of Islam to Modern Times, edited by James Kritzeck; Holt, Rinehart and Winston, New York, 1964.

An excellent anthology with introductions, short bibliography.

Aspects of Islamic Civilization as Depicted in the Original Texts, edited by A.J. Arberry; A.S. Barnes and Co., Inc., New York, 1964.

Good anthology of selections, with bibliography and index.

The Book of the Thousand Nights and a Night, translated by R.F. Burton; 1885. Reissued, "New York, Privately Printed for Subscribers Only," no date.

The seven-volume Bombay Edition, edited by Leonard C. Smithers, of the 1885 translation.

The Islamic Tradition, by John B. Christopher; Harper & Row, Publishers, New York, 1972.

Short, concise guide to the entire range of Islam. Annotated bibliography and index.

The Koran, translated by J.M. Rodwell, 1861. Reissued by J.M. Dent & Sons, Ltd., London, 1909.

The translation reads well in parts, and the notes, mainly borrowed from Sale's translation, are helpful. The Suras, however, have been rearranged in what Rodwell considered chronological order. The fault in this is that each Sura is made up of so many divergent parts written at various times that it is all but impossible to state the date or order. The arrangement also presents the book in a manner which is at variance with Islamic tradition and the manner in which it is understood within that tradition.

The Koran, translated by George Sale; Frederick Warne and Co., Ltd., New York, n.d.

An edition of the classic translation published in 1734, with an introduction by Edward Denison Ross. Does not contain the long introduction by Sale. Numerous notes and index.

The Koran: Commonly Called the Alcoran of Mohammed, translated by George Sale; J.W. Moore, Philadelphia, 1856.

The fifth edition, with the Preliminary Discourse of over 100 pages, which covers Islamic mythology and folklore. Numerous notes and index.

The Koran: Selected Suras, translated by Arthur Jeffrey; The Heritage Press, New York, 1958.

A beautiful edition of selected Suras arranged in a different order than the standard text. The notes, mainly borrowed from Sale, are at the back of the book. The introduction is helpful in placing the history of the Koran in Western thought.

The Life of Muhammad: Apostle of Allah, by Ibn Ishaq, translated by Edward Rehatsek, edited by Michael Edwardes; The Folio Society, London, 1964.

A shortened version of the earliest biographer whose work has survived, Ibn Ishaq, who was born some eighty-five years after the Hegira. The translation was presented to the Royal Asiatic Society, London, in 1898.

Modern Islamic Literature from 1800 to the Present, edited by James Kritzeck; Holt, Rinehart and Winston, New York, 1970.

Excellent anthology with introduction and commentaries. Selected references.

Muhammad and the Islamic Tradition, by Emile Dermenghem, translated by Jean M. Watt; Harper & Brothers, New York, 1958.

A short, illustrated guide with selected Islamic works. Also select bibliography, but no index.

The Portable Arabian Nights, edited by Joseph Campbell; The Viking Press, New York, 1952.

A one-volume abridgment with a long introduction and summaries of omitted material. The translation used is that of John Payne, issued in 1881.

The Qur'an, translated and edited by Richard Bell; T. & T. Clark, Edinburgh, 1937.

A two-volume edition with a critical rearrangement of the Suras. Extensive notes.

The Quran: The Eternal Revelation Vouchsafed to Muhammad the Seal of the Prophets, translated by Muhammad Zafrulla Khan; Curzon Press, London and Dublin, 1971.

A translation by a believer, with a long introduction, presenting the book as a religious experience. The introduction is basically fundamentalist in its approach to the subject, similar to editions of the Bible edited by Fundamentalist Christians. The translation is often awkward in its use of English construction.

Shorter Encyclopedia of Islam, edited by H.A.R. Gibb and J.H. Kramers, on behalf of the Royal Netherlands Academy. Photomechanical reprint by E.J. Brill and Luzac & Co., 1965.

Though called "shorter," this encyclopedia contains 670 double columns of small type, filled with nearly every facet of Islamic life and thought. The major problem is the transliteration of the entry names, which is not according to the generally accepted English spellings but is the editors' own system. Many articles, if searched out, contain numerous references to mythological subjects. The writing style, unfortunately, is dull and often confused.

Tales and Legends of Morocco, by Elisa Chimenti, translated by Arnon Benamy; Ivan Obolensky, Inc., New York, 1965.

A collection of tales simply told. Glossary.

Chapter 8: Greek Mythology

Ancient Greek Myths and Modern Drama, by Angela Belli; New York University Press, New York, 1969.

A short study of various modern plays based on Greek mythology. Bibliography.

The Classic Myths in English Literature and in Art, by Charles Mills Gayley; Ginn & Company, Boston, 1893.

Popular study based on Bulfinch's *Age of Fable* (1855). Commentary on the myths. Index.

Classical Mythology in Literature, Art and Music, by Philip Mayerson; Xerox College Publishing, Lexington, Mass., 1971.

Excellent, illustrated coverage of Greek and Roman mythology in relation to the arts. Bibliography and index.

Classical Myths, by May J. Herzberg; Allyn and Bacon, Inc., Boston, 1935.

Popular illustrated study. Glossary and index.

Classical Myths That Live Today, by Frances E. Sabin; Silver, Burdett and Co., New York, 1927.

Popular study of Greek and Roman mythology. Appendix, with Who's Who in classical mythology, and index.

The Complete Greek Tragedies, edited by David Greene and Richard Lattimore; The University of Chicago Press, Chicago, 1959.

A four-volume set of the complete works translated by various hands, with introductions.

Greek and Roman Religion, by Alain Hus; Hawthorn Books, Publishers, New York, 1962.

Study by a Catholic, and part of Section XV, "Non-Christian

Beliefs," of the *Twentieth Century Encyclopedia of Catholicism*. Select bibliography but no index.

Greek Mythology, by Felix Guirand; Paul Hamlyn, London, 1963.
Fully illustrated short text. Index.

The Greek Myths, by Robert Graves; George Braziller, Inc., New York, 1955.
A study of Greek myths with Graves's sometimes strained interpretations. Good reading. Index.

A Handbook of Greek Mythology, by H.J. Rose; Methuen & Co., Ltd., London, 1928.
Interesting study, numerous notes. Bibliography and indexes.

Metamorphoses, by Ovid, translated by Rolfe Humphries; Indiana University Press, Bloomington, 1964.
A spirited verse translation of the classic text on Greek and Roman mythology. Glossary and index.

The Metamorphoses of Ovid, translated by Mary M. Innes; Penguin Books, Baltimore, 1955.
A prose translation, somewhat stiff and very British, with introduction and index.

The Metamorphoses of Ovid, translated by Henry T. Riley; H.G. Bohn, London, 1851.
A literal prose translation with notes.

Mythology, by Edith Hamilton; Little, Brown and Co., Boston, 1949.
Popular study of Greek, Roman, and Nordic myths. Index.

Myths of Greece and Rome, by H.A. Guerber; American Book Company, New York, 1893.
A study with reference to literature and art. Glossary and index.

Ovid's Metamorphoses in Fifteen Books; Heritage Press, New York, 1961.
An edition of Ovid's masterwork, illustrated by Hans Erni, with a translation into heroic couplets done in the eighteenth century by John Dryden, Alexander Pope, Joseph Addison, William Congreve, and "other eminent hands."

The Religion of the Greeks and Romans, by C. Kerényi; Thames and Hudson, London, 1962.
A Jungian approach to Greek myth and religion. Index.

Shelley's Prometheus Unbound: A Variorum Edition, edited by Lawrence John Zillman; University of Washington Press, Seattle, 1959.
A full study of the play and myth. Bibliography and index.

Chapter 9: Nordic and Finnish Mythologies and Folklores

The Elder Edda: A Selection, translated by W.H. Auden and Paul B. Taylor; Random House, New York, 1967.
A poetic translation, with an introduction and notes. Glossary of names.

The Elder Edda and the Younger Edda, translated by Benjamin Thorpe and I.A. Blackwell; Norroena Society, London, 1907.
The Elder (or Poetic) Edda, translated into stiff prose by Thorpe, and *The Younger (or Prose) Edda*, translated by Blackwell. Glossary.

Faust: Parts One and Two, by Johann Goethe, translated by George Madison Priest; Alfred A. Knopf, New York, 1941
Excellent translation with notes and introduction.

Finno-Ugric and Siberian Mythology, by Uno Holmberg; Marshall Jones Company, 1916. Reissued by Cooper Square Publishers, Inc., New York, 1964.
In *The Mythology of All Races* (Volume 4). A long, dull, and confused account of the two mythologies containing vast amounts of information which has to be sorted out and arranged by the reader. The complexity of the subject accounts for some of the confusion, and poor writing style for the rest.

Folktales of Germany, edited by Kurt Ranke, translated by Lotte Baumann; The University of Chicago Press, 1966.
Excellent collection with notes and sources, part of the series *Folktales of the World*, under the editorship of Richard M. Dorson. Index.

Gods and Myths of Northern Europe, by H.R. Ellis Davidson; Penguin Books, Baltimore, 1964.
A short study with sources. Index.

Grimm's Household Tales, translated by Margaret Hunt; George Bell and Sons, London, 1884. Reissued by Singing Tree Press, Detroit, 1968.

A two-volume edition with Grimm's notes and an introduction by Andrew Lang.

Paths Through the Forest: A Biography of the Brothers Grimm, by Murray B. Peppard; Holt, Rinehart and Winston, New York, 1971.
A study covering every aspect of the brothers. Selected bibliography and index.

The Heroes of Asgard: Tales from Scandinavian Mythology, by A. and E. Keary; Macmillan and Co., New York, 1893.
A popular retelling of the myths and tales. Index of names.

Household Stories from the Collection of the Brothers Grimm, translated by Lucy Crane; Macmillan and Co., London, 1882. Reissued by University Microfilms, Inc., Ann Arbor, 1966.
A popular edition with illustrations by Walter Crane.

The Kalevala: The Epic Poem of Finland, translated by John Martin Crawford; The Robert Clarke Company, Cincinnati, 1904.
A two-volume edition of the epic, done in the original meter, using different spellings, however, of the major names than are used in other translations.

Kalevala: The Land of Heroes, translated by W.F. Kirby, introduction by J.B.C. Grundy; J.M. Dent & Sons, Ltd., London, 1907.
A two-volume edition of the epic done in the original meter. Often quite good, though the metrical scheme becomes somewhat tiring to read at length.

The Kalevala, or Poems of the Kaleva District, compiled by Elias Lönnrot, translated by Francis Peabody Magoun, Jr.; Harvard University Press, Cambridge, Mass., 1963.
A prose translation with an introduction and glossary, making it the best edition of the work available in English.

The Old Kalevala and Certain Antecedents, compiled by Elias Lönnrot, translated by Francis Peabody Magoun, Jr.; Harvard University Press, Cambridge, Mass., 1969.
An earlier edition of *The Kalevala compiled in* 1835, translated into prose, with glossary and introduction. A perfect companion to Magoun's translations of the 1849 *Kalevala*.

Marlowe: Doctor Faustus, a Casebook, edited by John Jump; Aurora Publishers, Nashville, 1969.

A collection of critical essays on the Faust legend and Marlowe's play.

The Works of Christopher Marlowe, edited by C.F. Tucker Brooke; Oxford University Press, London, 1910.

An edition containing all the plays, such as *Doctor Faustus*, as well as Marlowe's translations of Ovid, and the narrative poem *Hero and Leander*.

Myths of Northern Lands, by H.A. Guerber; American Book Company, New York, 1895.

A popular retelling with "special reference to literature and art." Glossary and index.

The Portable Nietzsche, edited and translated by Walter Kaufmann; The Viking Press, New York, 1954.

An anthology, with introduction, containing *Thus Spoke Zarathustra*, *Twilight of the Idols*, *The Antichrist*, and *Nietzsche Contra Wagner*.

Norse Mythology: Legends of Gods and Heroes, by Peter Andreas Munch; The American-Scandinavian Foundation, New York, 1927.

A translation by Sigurd Bernhard Hustvedt of a classic popular nineteenth-century study.

The Poetic Edda, translated by Henry Adams Bellows; American-Scandinavian Foundation, New York, 1923. Reissued by Biblo and Tannen, New York, 1969.

A complete translation with numerous notes and a long, though somewhat prejudiced, account of the work. Index.

Popular Tales from the Norse, by George Webbe Dasent; David Douglas, Edinburgh, 1888. Reissued by Grand River Books, Detroit, 1971.

A translation of fifty-nine Norwegian folktales from the *Norske Folke-eventyr* published by Peter Christen Asbjornsen and Jorgen Moe in 1843 and 1844 and expanded in 1852. The collection was also republished by Dover Publications in 1970 as *East O' the Sun and West O' the Moon*.

The Prose Edda: Tales from Norse Mythology, by Snorri Sturluson, translated by Jean I. Young; University of California Press, Berkeley, 1964.

A translation of sections of the work with an introduction and index.

Scandinavian Folk-Lore, edited and translated by William A. Craigie;

Alexander Gardner, London, 1896. Reissued by Singing Tree Press, Detroit, 1970.

A collection, selected and translated by Craigie, of documents relating to Scandinavian folklore, with notes and index.

Scandinavian Legends and Folk-Tales, by Gwyn Jones; Oxford University Press, London, 1956.

A popular retelling of many tales from various sources.

Scandinavian Mythology, by H.R. Ellis Davidson; Paul Hamlyn, London, 1969.

A good, concise, illustrated study with index.

The Sources of the Faust Tradition, edited by Philip Mason Palmer and Robert Pattison More; Oxford University Press, Ltd., London, 1936. Reissued by Octagon Books, New York, 1969.

A collection of documents on Faust serving as background to Goethe's *Faust*. Excellent source book with index.

Teutonic Myth and Legend, by Donald A. Mackenzie; The Gresham Publishing Co., London, n.d.

A retelling of Northern myths and sagas. Index.

Teutonic Mythology, by Jacob Grimm; George Bell and Sons, London, 1883. Reissued by Dover Publications, New York, 1966.

A four-volume study by the compiler of the Grimm folktales, often dull but filled with information. Index.

Transformations, by Anne Sexton; Houghton Mifflin Company, Boston, 1971.

A series of poems based on various folktales told by the Brothers Grimm.

Chapter 10: Slavic Mythologies and Folklores

Folktales of Hungary, edited by Linda Dégh, translated by Judit Hálasz; The University of Chicago Press, 1965.

An excellent collection of tales. The notes, however, tend to present the tales in the light of Communist philosophy, as the work was originally edited in Communist Hungary. Foreword by Richard M. Dorson.

Folk Tales from Russian Lands, translated and edited by Irina Zheleznova; Dover Publications, Inc., New York, 1969.

This is an unabridged republication of a work originally published by the Foreign Languages Publishing House, Moscow, in 1963, under the title *A Mountain of Gems: Fairy-Tales of the Peoples of the Soviet Land*. This variation of title expresses the markets each edition is trying to reach. Generally the tales are of less interest than other collections cited in the Bibliography.

Heroes of Serbia, by Nada Ćurčija-Prodanović; Oxford University Press, London, 1963. Illustrated by Dušan Ristić.

The Serbian ballads told in prose, giving some of the legends surrounding Dushan the Mighty as well as Kralyevich Marko.

Hungarian Classical Ballads and Their Folklore, by Ninon A. M. Leader; Cambridge University Press, London, 1967.

A collection of ballads with copious notes. The ballads are translated into prose and often rather awkward in phrasing. The notes, however, are very thorough and informative.

The Jolly Tailor and Other Fairytales Translated from the Polish, by Lucia Merecka Borski and Kate B. Miller; David McKay Company, Inc., New York, 1928. Illustrated by Kazimir Klepacki

A charming collection of tales told with wit and humor.

Krylov's Fables Translated into English Verse, translated by Bernard Pares; Harcourt, Brace and Co., New York, n.d.

A complete edition of one of the best-known writers of fables. With an introduction, but no index.

A Lermontov Reader, edited and translated by Guy Daniels; The Macmillan Company, New York, 1965.

A selection of the author's work, including a novel, *Princess Ligovskaya*, and the play *The Strange One* as well as a translation of *Thamar*.

Medieval Russia's Epics, Chronicals and Tales, edited by Serge A. Zenkovsky; A Dutton Paperback, E. P. Dutton, Inc., New York, 1974.

A massive collection of hard-to-find material, with an excellent introduction and notes, giving a complete translation of *The Lay of Igor's Army* in addition to generous selections from *The Tale of Bygone Years*.

Myths and Folktales of the Russians, Western Slavs and Magyars, by Jeremiah Curtin; Little, Brown and Co., Boston, 1890.

Interesting collection with notes and a good introduction.

Old Peter's Russian Tales, by Arthur Ransome; T.C. and E.C. Jack, Ltd.,

London, 1916. Reprinted by Dover Publications, Inc., New York, 1969.

Many of the tales are from Afanasiev's collection of Russian folktales, though the grim humor is softened by Ransome, and sometimes the endings of the tales are changed.

The Penguin Book of Russian Verse, edited by Dimitri Obolensky; Penguin Books, England, 1962.

Russian texts and prose translations at the bottom of the page. Contains *The Lay of Igor's Army*, some *Bylíny*, the *Dukhóvnye Stikhí*, as well as selections of Ivan Krylov, the fabulist.

The Works of Alexander Pushkin: Lyrics, Narrative Poems, Folk Tales, Plays, Prose, edited by Avrahm Yarmolinsky; Random House, New York, 1936.

A generous one-volume edition of Pushkin containing excerpts from *Poltava*, the complete *Tale of the Golden Cockerel*, and the play *Boris Godunov*. The volume also contains Pushkin's masterpiece, *Eugene Onegin*.

Russian Fairy Tales, translated by Norbert Guterman; Pantheon Books, Inc., New York, 1945. Illustrated by A. Alexeieff.

A collection based on Afanasiev's Russian folktales, with a folklorist commentary by Roman Jakobson and a good index. The best one-volume edition of Russian folktales in English.

Russian Folklore, by Y. M. Sokolov, translated by Catherine Ruth Smith; Folklore Associates, Hatboro, Pennsylvania, 1966. Introduction and bibliography by Felix J. Oinas.

A rather heavy-going Soviet approach to Russian and Soviet folklore by a noted Soviet scholar. It is very difficult to swallow lines like, "The poetry of the people is at present enveloped by the warm care of the Party, the Government, and the whole Soviet public."

Russian Wonder Tales, by Post Wheeler; Thomas Yoseloff, New York, "New Edition," 1957.

A selection of tales with twelve illustrations by Bilibin which make the book worthwhile.

Six Poems from the Russian, translated by Jacob Krup; The Galleon Press, New York, 1936. Twelve interpretive illustrations by Herbert Fouts.

The volume contains the complete *Poltava* by Pushkin and *The Demon* by Lermontov.

A.K. Tolstoy, by Margaret Dalton; Twayne Publishers, Inc., New York, 1972.

A short study which covers the major and minor works of one of the most important writers using Slavic folklore. Notes, selected bibliography, and index.

The Tragedy of Man: A Dramatic Poem in 15 Scenes, by Imre Madách, translated by Charles Henry Meltzer and Paul Vajda; Corvina, Budapest, 1933.

A long romantic play based on the Faust theme, using Adam as the hero.

A Treasury of Russian Literature, edited by Bernard Guilbert Guerney; The Vanguard Press, New York, 1943.

Excellent anthology, containing a complete version of the epic *The Lay of Igor's Army* as well as excerpts from the Ilya Muromets legends.

Chapter 11: Siberian Mythology and Folklore

Siberian Mythology, by Uno Holmberg; Marshall Jones Company, 1916. Reissued by Cooper Square Publishers, Inc., New York, 1964.

Volume 4 in the *Mythology of All Races* series. Notes and bibliography. No index except in the last volume of the thirteen-volume set.

Chapter 12: Hindu Mythology and Folklore

Hymns of the Atharva-Veda, translated by Maurice Bloomfield; Volume 42 of the *Sacred Books of the East;* Oxford University Press, 1897. Reprinted by Motilal Banarsidass, India, 1964.

The hymns, plus extracts from the ritual books and commentaries. There is a long introduction and numerous notes. The translation is somewhat awkward.

Bhagavadgita, the Sanatsugatiya and the Anugita, translated by Kashinath Trimbak Telang; Volume 8 of the *Sacred Books of the East;* Oxford University Press, 1882. Reprinted by Motilal Banarsidass, India, 1965.

Three important texts; the most important being the *Bhagavadgita.*

Bhagavad-Gita: The Song Celestial, translated by Edwin Arnold from the Sanskrit text into English verse; The Heritage Press, New York, 1965.

Contains an introduction by Shri Sri Prakasa and illustrations of paintings by Y.G. Srimati. A beautiful translation and edition of the classic Hindu religious writing.

A Classical Dictionary of Hindu Mythology and Religion, Geography, History and Literature, by John Dowson; Turbner's Oriental Series, Routledge & Kegan Paul, Ltd., 1878.
   Filled with information but written in a dry manner.

Dandin's Dasha-Kumara-Charita: The Ten Princes, translated by Arthur W. Ryder from the Sanskrit; The University of Chicago Press, Chicago, 1927.
   A modern translation of a classic Indian work.

The Fables of India, by Joseph Gaer; Little, Brown and Co., Boston, 1955.
   An excellent collection of tales from *The Panchantantra*, *The Hitopadesa*, and *The Jatakas*. There is a good introduction as well as an annotated bibliography.

The Five Sons of King Pandu: The Story of the Mahabharata, adapted from the English translation of Kisari Mohan Ganguli by Elizabeth Seeger. Illustrations by Gordon Laite. William R. Scott, Inc., New York, 1967.
   A necessarily cut one-volume telling of the epic with great charm.

Great Sanskrit Plays in Modern Translation, edited and translated by P. Lal; A New Directions Book, Norfolk, Conn., 1957.
   Versions of six plays: *Shakuntala*, *The Toy Cart*, *The Signet Ring of Rakshasa*, *The Dream of Vasavadatta*, *The Later Story of Rama*, and *Ratnavali*. Introduction, notes, and a pronouncing guide.

Hindoo Fairy Legends (Old Deccan Days), by Mary Frere; John Murray Publisher, circa 1881. Republished by Dover Publications, Inc., New York, 1967. With an introduction and notes by Bartle Frere; illustrations by Catherine Frances Frere.
   A popular collection which tends to be very Victorian in its phrasing, making some of the tales very dull as well as overly moralistic in outlook.

Hindu Literature, edited by Epiphanius Wilson; The Colonial Press, New York, 1900.
   An anthology containing *The Book of Good Counsels*, the "Nala and Damayanti" episode from the epic *Mahabharata*, the drama *Sakoontala*, and a shortened version of the *Ramayana*.

Hindu Mythology: Vedic and Puranic, by W.J. Wilkins; Curzon Press, London, and Rowman & Littlefield, Totowa, N.J., 1973.

This is the standard work first published in 1892 and reprinted in 1973. There are numerous quotations from Indian sources in the telling of the myths and legends, and in general, the information is presented in an interesting form. Illustrated and with an index.

Hindu Myths: A Sourcebook Translated from the Sanskrit, edited and translated by Wendy Doniger O'Flaherty; Penguin Books, Baltimore, 1975.

Excellent collection with good introduction. Selected bibliography, bibliographical notes, glossary, and index of proper names.

Hindu Scriptures, translated by R.C. Zaehner; Everyman's Library, London, 1966.

A selection of hymns from the *Rig-Veda,* the *Atharva-Veda,* the *Upanishads,* and the complete *Bhagavad-Gita.* Difficult reading, and a rather heavy translation of the texts. Zaehner's edition replaces the earlier Hindu Scriptures edited by Nicol Macnicol (1938), which had a different emphasis.

The Hindu World: An Encyclopedic Survey of Hinduism, by Benjamin Walker; Frederick A. Praeger, Publishers, New York, 1968.

A two-volume study in alphabetical arrangement, with emphasis on culture as opposed to mythology.

The Holy Lake of the Acts of Rama, edited and translated by W. Douglas, P. Hill; Oxford University Press, London, 1952.

A translation of Tulasi Das's *Ramacaritamanasa,* a retelling of the epic of Rama. Has an appendix listing the main characters.

The Hymns of the Rigveda, edited and translated by Ralph T.H. Griffith; 1896. Reissued by Motilal Banarsidass, Delhi, India, 1973.

A reissue, edited by J.L. Shastri, of a complete translation (with notes) of the hymns of the *Rig-Veda.* Appendixes; index of hymns according to deities and subjects; index of names.

Indian Fairy Tales, by Joseph Jacobs; David Nutt, London, 1892. Republished by Dover Publishers, Inc., New York, 1969. Illustrated by John D. Batten.

An interesting collection with notes and references at the back to show the relation of the tales to similar folktales throughout the world.

Indian Mythology, by Veronica Ions; Paul Hamlyn, London, 1967.

A concise, well-illustrated book on the complex subject. Aside from Hindu mythology, there is a section on Buddhist mythology and Jain mythology.

Institutes of Vishnu, translated by Julius Jolly; Volume 7 of the *Sacred Books of the East*; Oxford University Press, 1880. Reprinted by Motilal Banarsidass, India, 1965.

The *Vishnu-smriti*, or *Vaishnava Dharmasastra*, is a collection of ancient aphorisms on the sacred laws of India. Part One contains a discussion between the god Vishnu and the earth goddess.

The Laws of Manu, translated by G. Bühler; Volume 25 of the *Sacred Books of the East*; Oxford University Press, 1886. Reprinted by Motilal Banarsidass, India, 1964.

An important book of Hindu thought with a long introduction. Aside from the *Manu* text, it contains extracts from seven commentaries.

The Mahabharata, edited by Chakravarthi V. Narasimhan; Columbia University Press, 1965.

An English-language version based on selected verses with introduction, genealogical tables, glossary, and an index of verses on which the English prose version is based.

The Mahabharata of Krishna-Dwaipayana Vyasa, translated by Pratap Chandra Roy; reissued by Munshiram Manoharlal Publishers, India, 1974.

Complete translation in twelve volumes done in the last century and now reissued.

Myths and Legends of India, by Veronica Ions; Hamlyn Publishing Group, Ltd., London, 1970. Illustrated by Biman Mullick.

A collection of less familiar tales.

Myths and Symbols in Indian Art and Civilization, by Heinrich Zimmer, edited by Joseph Campbell; Princeton University Press, 1946.

A rather heavy-handed treatment of Indian mythology with a Jungian emphasis. There is an index and a collection of photos of Indian art works.

Poetical Works, by Edwin Arnold; Roberts Brothers, Boston, 1892.

A two-volume "complete" edition of the original poems and numerous translations of Arnold. Included are the complete translation of the *Gita Govinda*, the *Bhagavad-Gita*, called *The Song Celestial*, eight episodes from the epic poem *Mahabharata*, and assorted poems translated from the Sanskrit. Also included is *The Light of Asia*, a life of the Buddha in blank verse which was very popular in the nineteenth century.

Philosophies of India, by Heinrich Zimmer; Pantheon Books, New York, 1951.

A study of various mythologies and religions found in India. Bibliography and general index.

The Principal Upanisads, edited and translated by Radhakrishnan; Harper & Brothers, Publishers, New York, 1953.

A full text with translation, notes, and comments, with a book-length introduction. Difficult reading nevertheless.

The Ramayan of Valmiki, translated into English verse by Ralph T.H. Griffith; The Chowkhamba Sanskrit Series Office, India, 1963.

A reprint of the complete translation published between 1870 and 1875, with introduction and notes. The poetics of the translation often leave much to be desired.

The Ramayana of Valmiki, edited and translated by Hari Prasad Shastri; Shantisadan, London, 1962.

Complete prose translation of the epic in three volumes. Appendixes and glossaries.

The Religion of India, by Max Weber; The Free Press of Glencoe, 1958.

A study of the sociology of Hinduism and Buddhism. Notes and index.

The Upanishads, translated by F. Max Müller; Volumes 1 and 15 of the *Sacred Books of the East*; Oxford University Press, 1879 and 1884. Reprinted by Motilal Banarsidass, India, 1965.

A long introduction and twelve Upanishads in a stiff, awkward translation.

Vedanta-Sutras, translated by George Thibaut; volumes 34, 38, and 48 in the *Sacred Books of the East*, Oxford University Press, 1904. Reprinted by Motilal Banarsidass, India, 1962.

The *Vedanta-Sutras* with commentary by Sankaracarya and a book-length introduction in volumes 34 and 38. Volume 48 contains the *Vedanta-Sutras* with the commentary by Ramanuja.

Vedic Hymns, translated by Max Müller and Hermann Oldenberg, Volumes 32 and 46 in the *Sacred Books of the East;* Oxford University Press, 1891. Reprinted by Motilal Banarsidass, India, 1964.

Volume 32, with a long introduction and copious notes by Max Müller, contains hymns to the Maruts, Rudra, Vayu, and Vata. Volume 46 contains hymns to Agni. The translations in both cases are stiff and awkward.

Chapter 13: Buddhist Mythology and Folklore

The Buddha: Buddhist Civilization in India and Ceylon, by Trevor Ling; Charles Scribner's Sons, New York, 1973.

A modern life that attempts, not too successfully, to interpret the social and religious background of the time. Notes and index.

Buddha and the Gospel of Buddhism, by Ananada Coomaraswamy; 1916. Reissued by University Books, New Hyde Park, New York, 1964.

A popular, classic study of the entire field. Bibliography, glossary, and index.

Buddhism, by Christmas Humphreys; Penguin Books, Middlesex, England, 1951.

A short, popular study. Bibliography, glossary, and index.

Buddhism: The Light of Asia, by Kenneth K.S. Ch'en; Barron's Educational Series, Inc., Woodbury, N.Y., 1968.

A short study covering the whole range. Notes and glossary, selected bibliography and index.

Buddhism in Translations, edited and translated by Henry Clarke Warren; Harvard University Press, 1896. Reissued by Atheneum, New York, 1972.

A collection selected from Buddhist sources in Pali, with a selection of legends. No index.

The Buddhism of Tibet, or Lamaism, by L. Austine Waddell; W.H. Allen & Co., London, 1895. Reissued by Dover Books, New York, 1972 (called *Tibetan Buddhism*).

An illustrated, turn-of-the-century study of the "mystic cults, symbolism and mythology" of Tibetan Buddhism. Index.

A Buddhist Bible, edited by Dwight Goddard; George G. Harrap & Co., London, 1956.

A collection, in the words of the editor, that keeps "in mind the spiritual needs" of its readers. Little on legend. No index.

Buddhist Mahayana Tests, edited and translated by E.B. Cowell, F. Max Müller, and J. Takakusu; Volume 49 of the *Sacred Books of the East*; Oxford University Press, 1894. Reissued by Motilal Banarsidass, India, 1965.

A collection of various short texts with notes and introductions.

Buddhist Suttas, edited and translated by T.W. Rhys Davids; Volume 11 of the *Sacred Books of the East*; Oxford University Press, 1881. Reissued by Motilal Banarsidass, India, 1965.

A collection of various short texts translated from Pali, with an introduction and notes. Index.

Buddhist Texts Through the Ages, edited by Edward Conze; Bruno Cassier, Oxford, 1954. Reissued by Harper Torchbooks, New York, 1964.

A collection of texts from various sources. Bibliography and glossary.

The Dhammapada, translated by P. Lal; Farrar, Straus & Giroux, New York, 1967.

A translation from the Pali text with a good introduction. Select bibliography.

The Dhammapada and the Sutta-Nipata, edited and translated by F. Max Müller and V. Fausboll; Volume 10 of the *Sacred Books of the East*; Oxford University Press, 1881. Reissued by Motilal Banarsidass, India, 1965.

A translation from Pali, with long introductions and notes.

A Dictionary of Buddhism, by T.O. Ling; Charles Scribner's Sons, New York, 1972.

A rather difficult book to use, since it employs so many abbreviations. Little folklore or mythology. The text of the dictionary is taken from the Buddhist entries in *A Dictionary of Comparative Religion*, edited by S.G.F. Brandon (1970).

Entering the Path of Enlightenment, edited and translated by Marion L. Matics; The Macmillan Co., London, 1970.

A translation of the *Bodhicaryavatara* of the Buddhist poet Santideva from Sanskrit, written in the eighth century. Notes and glossary.

The Gods of Northern Buddhism, by Alice Getty; Oxford University Press, 1928. Reissued by Charles E. Tuttle Co., Rutland, Vermont, 1962.

A fully illustrated study of the history, iconography, and development of various Buddhist deities, with explanations of various foreign words, such as Sanskrit, used in the text. Index.

The Gospel of Buddha According to the Old Records, edited and translated by Paul Carus. Reissued by Omen Communications, Inc., 1972.

A reissue of a turn-of-the-century work containing texts translated and tied together by Carus. Excellent for legends. All the sources are identified. Glossary of names and terms.

The Jataka, or Stories of the Buddha's Former Births, edited by E.B. Cowell; 1895. Reissued by Cosmo Publications, India, 1973.

A six-volume set, translated by different hands, of all the fables, with notes. A must for the folklore of Buddhism. Index in Volume 6.

The Jatakamala: Garland of Birth-Stories of Aryasura, edited and translated by J.S. Speyer; 1895. Reissued by Motilal Banarsidass, India, 1971.

The Jataka tales according to the Northern Buddhists, containing thirty-four tales. Notes and index.

The Life of Buddha, by A. Ferdinand Herold, translated by Paul C. Blum; Albert & Charles Boni, New York, 1927.

A life "according to the legend of ancient India," containing interesting lore.

The Life of the Buddha, by H. Saddhatissa; Harper & Row, Publishers, New York, 1976.

A short life, drawn from various sources. Short bibliography and index.

The Light of Asia, or The Great Renunciation, by Edwin Arnold; Routledge & Kegan Paul, London, 1891.

A life of Buddha told in blank verse, extremely popular in the nineteenth century.

Notes on the Bauddha Rock-Temples of Ajanta Bombay, by James Burgess; printed by order of the Government at the Government Central Press, 1879. Reissued by Susil Gupta, Staten Island, New York, 1970.

An illustrated guide covering much mythology.

On the Eightfold Path: Christian Presence Amid Buddhism, by George Appleton; Oxford University Press, New York, 1961.

A short study of the relation between Buddhism and Christianity. Short bibliography and index.

Outlines of Mahayana Buddhism, by Daisetz Teitaro Suzuki; Luzac and Co., London, 1907. Reissued by Schocken Books, New York, 1963.
A very readable study, covering different aspects of the subject. Index.

A Popular Dictionary of Buddhism, by Christmas Humphreys; The Citadel Press, New York, 1962.
A short work, often helpful, though of little use for legends.

The Questions of King Milinda, edited and translated by T.W. Rhys Davids; volumes 25 and 26 of the *Sacred Books of the East;* Oxford University Press, 1894. Reissued by Motilal Banarsidass, 1965.
A basic text in Buddhism, with introduction, notes, and indexes.

The Saddharma-Pundartka, edited and translated by H. Kern; Oxford University Press, 1884. Reissued by Motilal Banarsidass, India, 1965.
A translation of *The Lotus of the True Law*, with introduction, notes, and index.

The Tantric Mysticism of Tibet, by John Blofeld; George Allen and Unwin Ltd., and E.P. Dutton, 1970. Reissued by Causeway Books, New York, 1974.
A study of the Buddhism of Tibet. Glossary and index.

The Teachings of the Compassionate Buddha, edited by E.A. Burtt; The New American Library, Mentor Books, 1955.
A short but good anthology on Buddhism, with commentary.

The Three Pillars of Zen, edited by Philip Kapleau; Beacon Press, Boston, 1965.
A book of texts with commentary of the "teaching, practice and enlightenment" of Zen. Zen vocabulary. Index.

The Tibetan Book of the Dead, edited by W.Y. Evans-Wentz; Oxford University Press, London, 1960.
A sacred collection, made by Evans-Wentz, called "The After-Death Experiences of the *Bardo* Plane, according to Lama Kazi Dawa-Samdup's English Rendering." Index.

Two Lamaistic Pantheons, by Walter Eugene Clark; Harvard University Press, 1937. Reissued by Paragon Book Reprint Corp., New York, 1965.

A one-volume edition of volumes 3 and 4 of the Harvard-Yenching Institute Monograph Series. Contains illustrations of deities with Sanskrit, Tibetan, and Chinese indexes of the various names.

Chapter 14: Chinese Mythology and Folklore

China and Religion, by Edward Harper Parker; E.P. Dutton & Co., New York, 1905.
A study of native beliefs and those adopted from other cultures, such as Christianity and Islam. Index.

Chinese Folktales, translated by Ewald Osers; G. Bell & Sons, London, 1971.
A fascinating collection originally published as *Chinesische Märchen*, translated into German by Richard Wilhelm, 1958. Notes.

Chinese Literature, edited by Epiphanius Wilson; The Colonial Press, New York, 1900.
An anthology, with introductions, containing *The Analects of Confucius, The Sayings of Mencius, The Shi-King, The Travels of Fa-Hien,* and the play *The Sorrows of Han.*

Chinese Mythology, by Anthony Christie; Paul Hamlyn, London, 1968.
A concise, illustrated guide to the complex field of Chinese mythology. Index.

Chinese Mythology, by John C. Ferguson; Volume 8 of *Mythology of All Races;* Jones Company, Boston, 1928. Reissued by Cooper Square Publishers, New York, 1964.
A short study, with numerous illustrations, giving a general view of the subject. Bibliography and index.

Chinese Religions from 1000 BC to the Present Day, by D. Howard Smith; Holt, Rinehart and Winston, New York, 1968. History of Religion Series, E.O. James, general editor.
A short study with notes, glossary, and index.

Chinese Symbols and Superstitions, by Harry T. Morgan; P.D. and Ione Perkins, California, 1942. Reissued by Gale Research Co., Book Tower, Detroit, 1972.
A short study, with 101 illustrations from Chinese sources, cover-

ing varying aspects of Chinese myth and legend. In general the study is rather superficial. Index.

Chinese Thought, by Paul Carus; Open Court, La Salle, Illinois, 1907. Reissued by Open Court, 1974 (abridged as *Chinese Astrology*).

Various aspects of Chinese belief, with a study of Confucius, Occultism, and examples of Filial Piety.

Confucius: The Man and the Myth, by H.G. Creel; John Day Co., New York, 1949. Reissued by Harper Torchbooks, New York, 1960, as *Confucius and the Chinese Way.*

Good, extensive study of Confucius with notes, references, bibliography, and index.

A Dictionary of Chinese Mythology, by E.T.C. Werner; Kelley and Walsh, Ltd., Shanghai, 1932. Reissued by The Julian Press, New York, 1961.

A standard work in the field, but one that must be used with extreme caution since it contains many mistakes. Bibliography.

The Folk-Lore of China and Its Affinities with That of the Aryan and Semitic Races, by N.B. Dennys; Trübner and Co., London, 1876. Reissued by Tower Books, Book Tower, Detroit, 1971.

An interesting work dealing with such subjects as birth, marriage, and death as well as superstitions, ghosts, witchcraft, and demonology. Index.

Folktales of China, edited by Wolfram Eberhard; University of Chicago Press, Chicago, 1965. Part of the series *Folktales of the World*, Richard M. Dorson, general editor.

Many of the tales of this newly edited volume were originally included in *Chinese Fairy Tales and Folk Tales;* collected and translated from the Chinese by Wolfram Eberhard; translated from the German by Desmond Parsons; and published by Kegan Paul, Trench, Trübner and Co., London, 1937. The present volume contains extensive notes to the tales, index of motifs, bibliography, and general index.

The Golden Casket: Chinese Novellas of Two Millennia, translated by Christopher Levenson; George Allen and Unwin, Ltd., London, 1965.

A brilliant collection of Chinese short literary works from Wolfgang Bauer's and Herbert Franke's German version of the original Chinese. List of sources. Notes.

Lao Tzu: Tao Te Ching, edited and translated by D.C. Lau; Penguin Books, Baltimore, 1963.

A modern translation with a long introduction, notes, and glossary.

Li Sao and Other Poems of Chu Yuan, translated by Yang Hsien-yi and Gladys Yang; Foreign Language Press, Peking, 1955.

A modern translation with a long introduction along Marxist lines. In this translation, "The Eleven Odes to Various Gods" often masks the mythological content.

Love and Protest, edited and translated by John Scott; Rapp and Whiting, Ltd., London, 1972. Reissued by Harper & Row, New York, 1972.

A modern translation, with an introduction, of Chinese poems from the sixth century BC to the seventeenth century AD.

Outlines of Chinese Symbolism and Art Motives, by C.A.S. Williams; Kelly and Walsh, Ltd., Shanghai, 1941. Reissued by Charles E. Tuttle Co., Rutland, Vermont and Tokyo, Japan, 1974.

This popular study, illustrated with line drawings from various sources, is an alphabetical listing of various legends, gods, customs, etc. Index.

Religion in a Chinese Town, by Philip Chesley Baity; The Chinese Association for Folklore, Taipei, Republic of China, 1975. Part of *Asian Folklore and Social Life Monographs*, Volume 64.

A scholarly study of present-day worship and beliefs. Glossary. References cited.

The Religion of China, by Max Weber; The Free Press of Glencoe, 1951.

A study of Confucianism and Taoism. Notes and index.

The Sacred Books of China, edited and translated by James Legge; Clarendon Press, Oxford, 1885. Volumes 3, 16, 27, 28, 39, and 40 of *Sacred Books of the East*. Reissued by Motilal Banarsidass, India, 1966.

These six volumes contain the texts of Confucianism and Taoism. The Confucian texts are the *Shu King*, the *Religious Portions of the Shi King*, the *Hsiao King*, the *Yi King*, and the *Ki Ki*. The Taoist texts are the *Tao Teh King*, the writings of *Kwang-Tze* (Chuang-Tsu), and the *Thai-Shang Tractate of Actions and Their Retributions*. Extensive notes, introductions, and various indexes in a rather stilted translation.

The Sacred Books of Confucius and Other Confucian Classics, edited and translated by Ch'u Chai and Winberg Chi; Bantam Books, Inc., 1965.

A work containing a long introduction, one part of which discusses Confucianism as a religion, as well as translations of Confucius, Mencius, Hsün Tzu, *Ta Hsüeh* ("The Great Learning"), *Chung Yung* ("The Doctrines of the Mean"), *Hsiao Ching* ("The Classic of Filial Piety"), and *Li Chi* ("The Book of Rites"), and Tung Chung-Shu. Glossary and index.

A Source Book of Chinese Philosophy, edited and translated by Wing-Tsit Chan; Princeton University Press, Princeton, New Jersey, 1963.

From ancient times to the present. Bibliography and index.

Translations from the Chinese, translated by Arthur Waley; Alfred A. Knopf, New York, 1919.

Brilliant translations of Chinese poems with introductory notes.

The White Pony, edited by Robert Payne; The John Day Co., New York, 1947.

An anthology of Chinese poetry from the earliest times, with a good introduction.

Chapter 15: Japanese Mythology and Folklore

Anthology of Japanese Literature, edited by Donald Keene; Grove Press, New York, 1955.

A two-volume selection of representative works including selections from the *Kojiki* and a No play, *Atsumori*, by Seami Motokiyo, based on an episode from the *Heike* epic.

The Arts of Shinto, by Haruki Kageymana, edited by Christine Guth; Weatherhill/Shibundo, New York/Tokyo, 1973.

A fully illustrated book giving the history, symbolism, and background of Shinto Japanese art. Volume 4 of the *Arts of Japan*.

Gods of Myth and Stone: Phallicism in Japanese Fold Religion, by Michael Czaja; Weatherhill, Tokyo/New York, 1974.

A very thorough study of various Shinto gods worshiped in Japan, with excellent illustrations, notes, and bibliography.

Historical and Geographical Dictionary of Japan, by E. Papinot; Frederick Ungar Publishing Co., New York, 1964.

A reissue of the 1910 English edition of this two-volume study of various aspects of Japanese life. The mythological and folkloric entries, however, are not very thorough.

History of Japanese Religion, by Masaharu Anesaki; Kegan Paul, Trench, Trübner & Co., London, 1930. Reissued by Charles E. Tuttle Co., Vermont and Tokyo, 1963.

Considered by some scholars a "classic in its field," the volume gives a rather complete study of Shinto beliefs.

The Japanese Fairy Hook, compiled by Yei Theodora Ozaki; Archibald Constable & Co., Ltd., 1903. Reissued by Dover Pbulications, New York, 1967.

An excellent collection of folktales compiled at the suggestion of Andrew Lang, the great compiler of folktales in the nineteenth century.

Japanese Grotesqueries, compiled by Nikolas Kiej'e; Charles E. Tuttle Co., Rutland, Vermont/Tokyo, Japan, 1973.

A collection of prints of Japanese demons and spirits, with short comments. There is a long introduction by Terence Barrow which is quite helpful.

Japanese Mythology, by Juliet Piggott; Paul Hamlyn, London, 1969.

A short study with many illustrations of Japanese mythology and legend, forming a good introduction to the subject.

Japan's Religions: Shinto and Buddhism, edited by Kazumitsu Kato; University Books, Inc., New York, 1966.

An excellent selection of various works by Lafcadio Hearn relating to Japanese Shinto and Buddhist beliefs, practices, etc. Helpful index.

Kojiki, edited and translated by Donald L. Philippi; Princeton University Press, University of Tokyo Press, 1969.

A modern, up-to-date translation of a classic text on Japanese mythology, with a long introduction and glossary of over 200 pages. A must.

Ko-Ji-Ki: Records of Ancient Matters, edited and translated by Basil H. Chamberlain; Lane, Crawford & Co., Kelly & Co., Yokohama, 1883.

One of the main original sources for Japanese mythology in a rather stiff translation that avoids the "obscene" passages of the work.

Kwaidan: Stories and Studies of Strange Things, by Lafcadio Hearn; The Shimbi Shoin, Ltd., Tokyo, 1932 (for the Limited Editions Club). Reissued by Dover Publications, New York, 1968.

A classic collection of Japanese ghost tales with an introduction by Oscar Lewis and illustrations by Yasumasa Fujita.

Legend in Japanese Art, by Henri L. Joly; John Lane The Bodley Head, London, 1908. Reissued by Charles E. Tuttle Co., Vermont/Tokyo, 1967.

An A-to-Z listing of over a thousand figures, etc., from myth, legend, and folklore in Japan, with 700 illustrations. Generally an invaluable guide, though weak in entries on mythology.

Nihongi: Chronicles of Japan from the Earliest Times to AD 697, edited and translated by W. G. Aston; Kegan Paul, Trench, Trübner & Co., London, 1896. Reissued by Allen and Unwin, London, 1956.

An original book of Japanese mythology, forming with the *Kojiki* the main source for the study of Japanese mythology.

The Selected Writings of Lafcadio Hearn, edited by Henry Goodman; The Citadel Press, 1949.

A selection of works by Hearn, such as *Kwaidan*, his Japanese ghost tales, *Some Chinese Ghosts*, plus other works, including *Stories of Japanese Life*. There is an introduction by Malcolm Cowley.

The Seven Lucky Gods of Japan, by Reiko Chiba; Charles E. Tuttle Co., Vermont/Tokyo, Japan, 1966.

A short, popular study of the subject, with contemporary illustrations.

Shinto: The Kami Way, by Dr. Sokyo Ono; Charles E. Tuttle Co., Rutland, Vermont/Tokyo, Japan, 1962.

A concise stydy of present-day Shinto belief with background of its development.

Shinto: The Unconquered Enemy, by Robert O Ballou; The Viking Press, New York, 1945.

"Japan's doctrine of racial superiority and world conquest with selections from Japanese texts." Notes, annotated bibliography, and recommendations for further reading. Index.

Tales of Old Japan, by Lord Redesdale; Macmillan and Co., Ltd., London, 1908 edition.

One of the best collections of Japanese tales with illustrations, originally issued in 1871.

The Three Treasures: Myths of Old Japan, by Miriam Cox; Harper & Row, New York, 1964.

A retelling of myths from the *Kojiki* and the *Nihongi* with contemporary illustrations by Kingo Fujii and explanations of the meanings of the Japanese myths in relation to Greek mythology.

Chapter 16: African Mythologies and Folklores

African Folklore, edited by Richard Dorson; Doubleday, 1972.

Scholarly treatment of folklore concepts applied to the oral traditions of Africa. Contains essays which emerged from the Folklore Institute of Indiana University.

African Mythology, by Geoffrey Parrinder; Paul Hamlyn Group, Ltd., London, 1967, 1969.

A particularly valuable book for those not familiar with the vast scope of mythology and lore produced by Africans. Of necessity, the work is selective in terms of the groups whose tales are covered. Highly professional presentation of African art.

Dictionary of Black African Civilization, by Georges Balindier, Jacques Maquet, et al.; Leon Amiel, New York, 1974.

Clear, simple entries in a richly illustrated work. Highly praised in its 1968 French edition, the English version is more up to date.

Fourteen Hundred Cowries and Other African Tales, by Abayomi Feya; Washington Square Press, New York, 1971.

Detailed retellings of the Yoruba people's West African tales. Original illustrations expressive of African culture.

Myths and Legends of Africa, by Margaret Carey; Paul Hamlyn, London, 1970.

An excellent retelling of some African tales. Good general introduction. Illustrated.

Profiles in Ethnology, by Elman R. Service; Harper & Row, 1958.

Highly selective, in-depth, secondary treatment of several primitive tribes. The chapters dealing with Africa are particularly useful to the student of African mythology.

Tales of Yoruba Gods and Heroes, by Harold Courlander; Fawcett Publications, Inc., 1974.
   Intelligent collection of Yoruba folklore.

Chapter 17: North American Indian Mythologies

The Algonquin Legends of New England, or Myths and Folk Lore of the Micmac, Passamaquoddy, and Penobscot Tribes, edited by Charles G. Leland; Houghton, Mifflin and Co., Boston, 1884. Reissued by Singing Tree Press, Detroit, 1968.
   A classic collection of tales with explanations of their relationship to other mythologies and folklores. The problem with these tellings is that the English is quite stilted and unnatural.

American Indian Legends, by Vladimir Hulpach; Paul Hamlyn, London, 1965.
   A general collection put into a narrative framework.

American Indian Legends, edited by Allan A. Macfarlan; The Heritage Press, New York, 1968.
   A varied collection, mainly from literary sources, including creation myths; hero and culture-hero tales; legends of little people, giants, and monsters; tales of mystery, medicine, and magic; and Trickster and transformation myths.

American Indian Mythology, edited by Alice Marriott and Carol K. Rachlin; Thomas Y. Crowell Co., New York, 1968. Reissued by Mentor, New York, 1972.
   An excellent collection, mainly from oral sources. Bibliography.

The Crow Indians, by Robert H. Lowie; Holt, Rinehart and Winston, 1935.
   A study with chapters devoted to religion, rites, festivals, the sacred pipe dance, and the sun-dance. Appendices, glossary, and index.

Dictionary of the American Indian, by John Stoutenburgh, Jr.; Philosophical Library, New York, 1960.
   A short dictionary giving concise information on tribes, etc. No entries for mythological figures or legends.

God Is Red, by Vine Deloria, Jr.; Grosset & Dunlap, New York, 1973.

A leading contemporary Indian spokesman offers an alternative to Christianity through a return to native Indian beliefs and concepts. Index.

Indian Masks and Myths of the West, by Joseph H. Wherry; Funk & Wagnalls, New York, 1969.
An interesting, helpful, and understanding account with illustrations. Bibliography, index of mythical beings, and general index.

The Indians' Book: Songs and Legends of the American Indians, edited by Natalie Curtis; Harper & Brothers, New York, 1923. Reissued by Dover Publications, New York, 1968.
A collection arranged according to the different sections and tribes in the United States. Index.

Indians of the Northeast Coast, by Philip Drucker; McGraw-Hill Book Company, Inc., New York, 1955.
A general study with chapters on religion and ceremonial. Bibliography and index.

Indians of the Plains, by Robert H. Lowie; McGraw-Hill Book Company, Inc., New York, 1954.
A study with chapters on Indian beliefs and ceremonies. Bibliography and index.

Letters and Notes on the Manners, Customs, and Conditions of the North American Indians (1832–1839), by George Catlin; Dover Publications, New York, 1973.
This edition of the classic nineteenth-century work is an unabridged republication of the London edition of 1844. It contains an introduction by Marjorie Halpin, which was first published in 1965 by The Smithsonian Institution. 2 volumes. No index.

Longhouse Legends, by Emerson N. Matson; Thomas Nelson & Sons, New Jersey, 1968.
A collection of tales of the Pacific Northwest Indians based on tellings by Chief Martin Sampson. Short bibliography.

The Myth of Hiawatha and Other Oral Legends, Mythologic and Allegoric of the North American Indians, edited by Henry R. Schoolcraft; J.B. Lippincott & Co., Philadelphia, 1856. Reissued by Kraus Reprint Co., New York, 1971.
One of the first collections of Indian myths and legends. School-

craft, however, made the mistake of identifying Hiawatha, the historical personage, with the god Manabozho.

Myths of the Modocs: Indian Legends of the Northwest, edited by Jeremiah Curtin; Boston, 1912. Reissued by Benjamin Blom, Inc., New York, 1971.

A classic collection made by one of the great collectors. Notes.

The Myths of the New World: A Treatise on the Symbolism and Mythology of the Red Race of America, by Daniel G. Brinton; David McKay, Philadelphia, 1896. Reissued by Gale Research Co., Detroit, 1974.

A pioneer study made by one of the most respected scholars of the last century. It deals with both North and South American mythology. Indexes.

North American Indian Mythology, by Cottie Burland; Hamlyn Publishing Corp., London, 1965.

An excellent short, illustrated volume on the subject. Bibliography and index.

North American Mythology, by Hartley Burr Alexander; Marshall Jones Company, 1916. Reissued by Cooper Square Publishers, New York, 1964. Volume 10 of *The Mythology of All Races.*

A discussion of North American mythology by area, such as the Far North, the forest tribes, the Gulf Region, etc. Notes, bibliography, and index.

Pomo Indian Myths and Some of Their Sacred Meanings, edited by Cora Clark and Texa Bowen Williams; Vantage Press, Inc., New York, 1954.

A collection of myths as well as Indian explanations of their meanings.

The Portable North American Indian Reader, edited by Frederick W. Turner; Viking Press, New York, 1973.

An excellent collection with over two hundred pages devoted to myths and legends. Bibliography.

The Sacred Pipe: Black Elk's Account of the Seven Rites of the Oglala Sioux, edited by Joseph Epes Brown; University of Oklahoma Press, 1953. Reissued by Penguin Books, Inc., Baltimore, 1971.

An account of the Sioux religion by one of its leading men. Index.

Seeing with a Native Eye: Essays on Native American Religion, edited by Walter Holden Capps; Harper & Row, New York, 1976.

A collection of essays by various people on different phases of North American Indian belief. Bibliography.

Shaking the Pumpkin: Traditional Poetry of the Indian North Americas, edited by Jerome Rothenberg; Doubleday & Co., New York, 1972.
    An excellent anthology giving native poetry with extensive commentaries.

Tales of the North American Indians, edited by Stith Thompson; Indiana University Press, Bloomington, 1929.
    A varied collection of tales including mythological stories, mythical incidents, Trickster tales, hero tales, journeys to the other world, animal wives and husbands, miscellaneous tales, tales borrowed from Europeans, and tales based on Bible stories. Notes and bibliography.

This Country Was Ours: A Documentary History of the American Indian, edited by Virgil J. Vogel; Harper & Row, New York, 1972.
    Useful for background on the life of the Indians. Bibliography and index.

The Trickster: A Study in American Indian Mythology, edited by Paul Radin; Philosophical Library, New York, 1956.
    A very helpful text giving the myth of the Trickster as well as commentaries by Karl Kerényi and C.G. Jung on its meaning.

Chapter 18: Aztec, Mayan, and Inca Mythologies

An Account of the Conquest of Guatemala in 1524, by Pedro De Alvarado; The Cortes Society, New York, 1924.
    A classic study. Notes and bibliography. Translated by Sedley J. Mackie.

American Hero-Myths: A Study in the Native Religions of the Western Continent, by Daniel G. Brinton; H.C. Watts & Co., Philadelphia, 1882. Reissued by Johnson Reprint Corp., New York, 1970.
    A brilliant, often enlightening treatment of the subject by one of the greatest authorities in the nineteenth century, who is still respected by scholars today.

The Ancient Maya, by Sylvanus Griswold Morley; Stanford University Press, Stanford, Calif., 1946.
    Excellent guide to the religion of the Mayas. Notes, bibliography, and index.

The Art of the Ancient Maya, by Alfred Kidder II and Carlos Samayoa Cinchilla; Thomas Y. Cromwell Co., New York, 1959.
Short study with many illustrations. No index.

Aztecs of Mexico, by George C. Vaillant; Doubleday, Doran & Co., Inc., 1944. Reissued by Penguin Books, 1966.
The origin, rise, and fall of the Aztecs. Notes, bibliography, and index.

The Conquest of the Incas, by John Hemming; Harcourt Brace Jovanovich, New York, 1970.
A full study, with glossary, bibliography, notes, and index.

Cortés, by Francisco López de Gómaru; University of California Press, 1964.
A translation from the *Istoria de la Conquista de Mexico* of 1552 by Lesley Byrd Simpson. Glossary and index.

The Discovery of Yucatan, by Francisco Hernández de Córdoba; The Cortes Society, 1942.
A basic original-source book. Translated from the original texts with introduction, notes, and index by Henry R. Wagner.

General History of the Things of New Spain, by Fray Bernardino de Sahagún; The University of Utah, 1955.
A classic work in thirteen parts translated from the Aztec into English. Notes.

The Gods of Mexico, by C.A. Burland; Eyre & Spottiswoode, London, 1967.
A concise and informative treatment of a complex subject by an authority. Contains a short annotated bibliography and an index.

The History of the Incas, by Alfred Métraux; Pantheon Books, New York, 1969.
A short, illustrated study. Bibliography. No index.

History of the Indians of New Spain, by Fray Toribio de Motolinía; Academy of American Franciscan History, Washington, D.C., 1951.
Classic work translated and annotated by Francis Borgia Steck. Bibliography and index.

The History of the Indies of New Spain, by Fray Diego Durán; Orion Press, New York, 1964.
A classic account translated with notes by Doris Heyden and Fernando Horcasitas. Bibliography and index.

Incidents of Travel in Central America, Chiapus and Yucatan, by John L. Stephens; Rutgers University Press, New Brunswick, 1949.

A nineteenth-century work edited with an introduction and notes by Richard L. Predmore. No index.

Latin America: A Cultural History, by Germón Arciniegas; Alfred A. Knopf, New York, 1968.

A study of the complex field. Bibliography and index.

Latin-American Civilization: Colonial Period, by Bailey W. Diffie; Octagon Books, New York, 1967.

Long, general study. Bibliography and index.

Lords of Cuzco: A History and Description of the Inca People in Their Final Days, by Burr Cartwright Brundage; University of Oklahoma Press, 1967.

A sympathetic study. Notes and index.

The Maya, by Michael D. Coe; Frederick A. Praeger, New York, 1966.

Illustrated short study. No bibliography. Index.

Maya: The Riddle and Rediscovery of a Lost Civilization, by Charles Gallenkamp; David McKay Co., Inc., New York, 1959.

Short study. Bibliography and index.

Maya Cities, by Paul Rivet; G.P. Putnam's Sons, New York, 1960.

An illustrated study with index.

Mexican Folkways, by Frances Toor; Crown Publishers, New York, 1947.

Excellent volume of customs, myths, folklore, traditions, etc. Glossary and index.

Popul Vuh: The Sacred Book of the Ancient Quiché Maya, edited and translated by Delia Goetz and Sylvanus G. Morley; University of Oklahoma Press, 1950.

An English version by the editors based on the translation of Andrián Recinos. The book is one of the most important documents for the mythology of the Maya. This edition contains a long introduction, numerous notes, and an index.

The Rise and Fall of Maya Civilization, by J. Eric S. Thompson; University of Oklahoma Press, 1954.

Excellent study. Bibliography and index.

The Spanish Empire in America, by C.H. Haring; Harcourt Brace & World, New York, 1947.
General study. Good bibliography, plus index.

Chapter 19: Voodoo Mythology and Folklore

Divine Horsemen: Voodoo Gods of Haiti, by Maya Deren; Chelsea House Publishers, New York, 1970.
A book written under the influence of Joseph Campbell and Jungian theories. Often interesting, though it leaves much unsaid regarding the Voodoo cults.

Secrets of Voodoo, by Milo Rigaud; translated by Robert B. Cross from the French; Arco, New York, 1969. Photographs by Odette Mennesson-Rigaud.
A sympathetic and interesting treatment of the subject, though the book lacks an index, which makes it difficult to locate some information.

Voodoo Secrets from A to Z, by Robert W. Pelton; A.S. Barnes and Co., South Brunswick, 1973.
A short A-to-Z listing of Voodoo terms. Helpful for quick reference.

Index